Sweetie Pie

Sweetie

EDITORIAL DEVELOPMENT BY DAVID RICKETTS

ART DIRECTION AND DESIGN BY BARBARA MARKS

Pie

CREATED BY RICHARD SIMMONS

THE
RICHARD SIMMONS
PRIVATE
COLLECTION
OF
DAZZLING
DESSERTS

GT
PUBLISHING
NEW YORK

Produced by Richard Simmons, David Ricketts, and Barbara Marks

Editorial Development
David Ricketts
Art Direction and Design
Barbara Marks

Recipe Development
Richard Simmons
Winifred Morice
Michael Krondl
Recipe Development Coordinator
Michael Krondl
Recipe Testers
JoAnn Brett
Catherine Chatham
Ruth Cousineau
Linda Dann
Sandra Rose Gluck
Terry Grieco Kenny
Elaine Khosrova
Maureen Luchejko
Frank Melodia
Paul Piccuito
Sarah Reynolds
Grace Young
Winifred Morice's Assistant
Lynda Hammersmith

Nutrition Editor
Susan M. McQuillan
Nutrition Analysis
Patti Santelli
Copy Editor and Proofreader
Stephen R. Frankel
Recipe Copy Editor
Janet Charatan
Proofreader
Jessica Cunningham

Food Photographer
Mark Thomas
Assistant
John Muggenborg
Food Stylist
Dora Jonassen
Assistant
Michael Pederson
Prop Stylist
Nancy Micklin

Photographer (Cover and Chapter Openers)
Ed Ouellette
First Assistant
Keith Leman
Assistants
Wolfgang Baeumle
Johann Pieders
Melinda Wilson
Food Stylist (Cover)
Karen Gillingham
Assistant
Stormie Ingram
Prop Stylist (Chapter Openers)
Sandra Wood

Poetry
Winifred Morice

Richard Simmons Wardrobe
Leslie Wilshire
Richard Simmons Makeup
Sheree Morgan
Richard Simmons Hair
Jimmy Grote

Prepress
Isle Graphic Associates
GGS Information Systems

Produced by Richard Simmons, David Ricketts, and Barbara Marks
Food photography by Mark Thomas

Published by GT Publishing Corporation
16 East 40th Street, New York, NY 10016

Library of Congress Cataloging-in-Publication Data

Simmons, Richard.
   Sweetie pie : the Richard Simmons private collection of dazzling desserts / by Richard Simmons.
      p.   cm.
   Includes index.
   ISBN 1-57719-276-1 (hardcover)
   1. Desserts.   I. Title.
   TX773.S523   1997
   641.6'8—dc21   97-34532
                                                              CIP

ISBN: 1-57719-276-1

Printed in the United States of America

10 9 8 7 6 5 4 3 2 1

First Printing

Contents

I dedicate this book
to the Cayre Family—
thank you for letting
all my soufflés rise!

OH YES–I HAVE SWEETIE PIES IN MY LIFE, BUT I ALSO HAVE SWEETIE PEOPLE.
MY LOVE TO ALL YOU SUGAR CUBES:

SHIRLEY SIMMONS	TOM KLUSARITZ	JIM GROTE
LEONARD SIMMONS	**CHRIS SNOOK**	ELIJAH JONES
	ANDY GREENBERG	**MARILYN LAMAS**
DAVID RICKETTS	**LYNN HAMLIN**	
BARBARA MARKS	KAREN WOLF	**MICHAEL CATALANO**
	GINA SANTANASTASIO	RICK BRADLEY
WINIFRED MORICE		**RICK HERSH**
ED OUELLETTE	**TOM ESTEY**	TERESA REVELES
KEITH "SWING MAN" LEMAN	MARGARET MCALLISTER	
KAREN GILLINGHAM	ALL MY FRIENDS AT PTA	**LESLIE WILSHIRE**
STORMIE & INGRID INGRAM		**SHEREE MORGAN**
SANDRA WOOD		JEFF KAMINSKI
MARK THOMAS		**ASHLEY, MELANIE, HATTIE,**
JOHN MUGGENBORG		**AND DOLLY**
DORA JONASSEN		
MICHAEL PEDERSON		
NANCY MICKLIN		

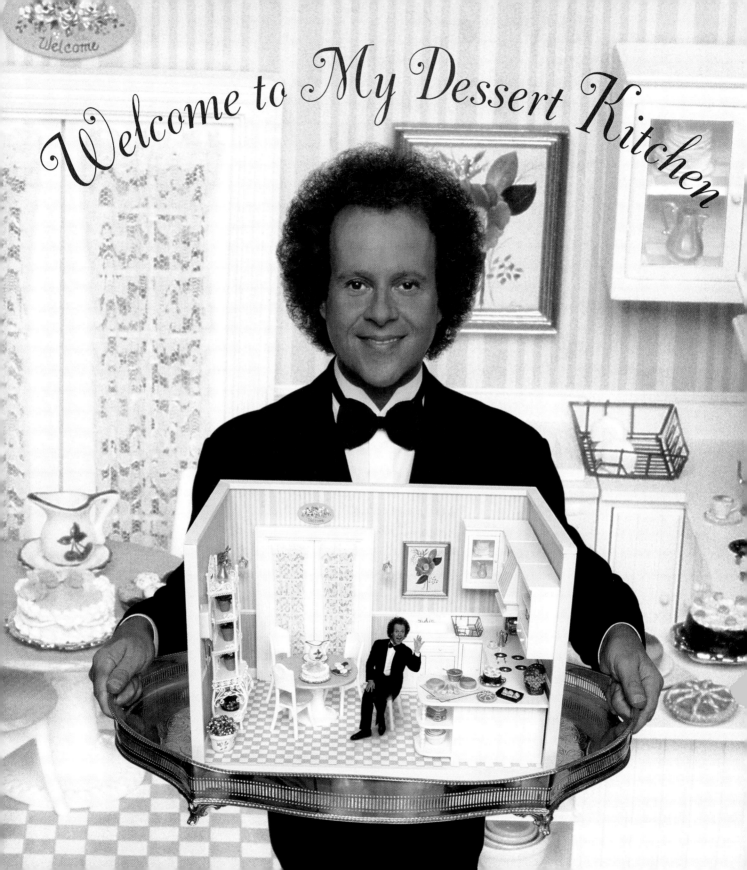

Welcome to My Dessert Kitchen

Some things are so special that they need a sacred space,
And for me it's in my kitchen, in a secret locked-up place.
Here I have released the lock, so all of you can see
How I treat my sweet tooth when it catches up with me.

Instead of looking outward for an instant sugar high
Or bathing in hot chocolate till the mood has passed me by,
I open up my cupboards with a password and a key,
And "Riccardo the Dessert Chef" is creatively set free.

The results of these adventures I present for you to taste
In regulated portions so as not to hurt your waist.
You'll only do it sometimes, on a special kind of day
Or on those rare occasions when your sweet tooth comes to play.

So welcome to my kitchen, where desserts are made with flair
And presented with an awesome hush that permeates the air.
Take the time to marvel and savor each effect,
Remembering that all desserts be handled with respect.

esserts! We all love them. Without them, life would be like an unending aerobics class. Don't get me wrong, aerobics is one of my favorite things. But we need something luscious and sweet in our lives every now and then. And that's why I've created *Sweetie Pie*.

After I finished my last book, *Farewell to Fat*, and was traveling around the country making recipes for people and talking about how to lower fat in cooking, I noticed people always wanted to know about desserts. Big surprise, right?

So when I returned home to L.A. between trips, I began thinking about another cookbook. Should it be hors d'oeuvres? Casseroles? Vegetables? Snacks? Nah. Desserts—that's what it will be! But these will be my very special desserts—the ones I love, and with fewer calories and less fat than their traditional counterparts.

How did I do it? Well, it wasn't easy. The toughest part was not eating all the leftovers as we developed these recipes. Portion control. Just because there's a whole *My, Oh My! Chocolate Mousse Pie* (pictured above; recipe, page 92) sitting in front of you, doesn't mean you have to eat the whole thing to make sure it tastes good. One slice, and even just one taste, will tell you that.

But there's another much more difficult task when it comes to reduced-fat desserts, especially in baking. And that's getting the amount of sugar and fat just right. If you don't, you wind up with something that tastes and chews like cardboard, rather than something that floated down from a cloud. It's all just one big chemistry lesson. Fortunately, I took very good notes when watching Mr. Wizard on TV as a boy, so I've done all the work for you. And sometimes it has taken a lot of tries to get it perfect. For this book, my theme song has been, "What a difference a tablespoon makes, 3 little teaspoons . . ."

LOW VS. REDUCED

Let me go over one important point with you. Although some of my recipes are low-fat and low-calorie, they are all reduced-fat, and most are reduced-calorie. What does that mean? Low-fat, according to the people in Washington, D.C. who decide such things, means 3 grams of fat or less per serving. Reduced-fat means a recipe has to have at least 25 percent less fat per serving when compared with a similar food. Got it? Low-calorie means 40 calories or less per serving—but forget that when it comes to desserts! And reduced-calorie is the same as reduced-fat—25 percent fewer calories per serving when compared to a similar food. To help you understand these differences, take a look at the following chart:

LOW-CALORIE	REDUCED-CALORIE
40 calories or less per serving	25% fewer calories per serving, when compared to similar food

LOW-FAT	REDUCED-FAT
3 g of fat or less per serving	25% less fat per serving, when compared to similar food

The calorie culprits: fat and sugar

Repeat after me: Desserts equal fat and sugar, and fat and sugar equal calories. Repeat 10 times.

CALORIES

When calories are good, they are very, very good. We need calories because they fuel our bodies so we can walk, run, jump, exercise, dance, and anything else we want. Where do calories come from? Fat and carbohydrates as well as protein. (I won't talk about protein here, since you don't get a lot of it in desserts.) But back to our story.

When calories are ___, they are very, very ___. You know what I mean. (There are certain words I don't like to say out loud when I'm talking about food.) But the point is, if we take in more calories than the body needs to keep the engine running, the excess goes immediately into fat-storage, without passing go.

FAT

So here we go. Let's start with fat. It's one of those things—you can't live with it, and you can't live without it. To stay healthy, we need to take in about 20 grams of fat from food every day. Why? In addition to providing energy, fat dissolves certain vitamins (A, D, E, and K) and distributes them throughout the body—it's like watering your garden. And we all know what happens when winter approaches—we get that little layer of extra fat to insulate us against the cold. It's our bodies' long underwear.

SUGAR

Now, what about carbohydrates? All carbos have something in common—sugar. You may already know there are simple carbohydrates and complex carbohydrates. Simple carbohydrates are what you practically always find in desserts, and that means plain old granulated table sugar and other sweeteners, such as honey. Simple sugars provide energy, but without any other nutrients. You've probably heard the phrase "empty calories." Well, that's what I'm talking about. So the key here is moderation. Eat a lot of sugar, and you put on the pounds, with no other redeeming benefits. In fruit, you find complex carbohydrates, and they provide not only energy, but a bonus—vitamins, minerals, and fiber. So any time you can put fruit in a dessert, as I do in my *Martha's Cherry-Pear Cobbler* (page 158), you get energy with some other good stuff. Got all that? Go back and review if you need to. We have the time—no rush. The important lesson to remember is, when you're talking desserts, keep an eye on the calories and the grams of fat.

Martha's Cherry-Pear Cobbler

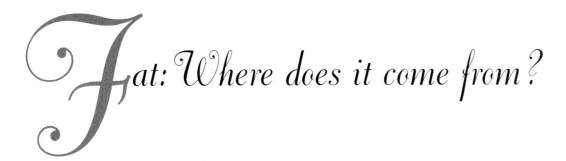

Fat: Where does it come from?

Where to begin? At the beginning, with the three different kinds of fat.

SATURATED FAT

This is the one you want to stay away from. Too much saturated fat leads to pounds of extra weight and has been tied to increased amounts of cholesterol in your bloodstream. Ugh! And that can mean heart and circulatory problems. Sorry to get so clinical, but you need to know. Where do you find saturated fat? In foods that come from animals—butter, eggs, milk, heavy cream, cheese, chocolate. (What—a chocolate cow? No, it's the cocoa butter in the cocoa bean). Saturated fat is also found in some plant products, such as shredded coconut and solid vegetable shortening.

One other thing—**CHOLESTEROL.** It comes from things that swim, fly, walk, and run—and not from plants.

POLYUNSATURATED AND MONOUNSATURATED FATS

These fats are okay, but that doesn't mean you can go crazy over them. We're still talking calories here. Polyunsaturated fat is found in lots of food, including vegetable oils such as sunflower, corn, soybean, and safflower. These are the oils you'll find in many of the butter substitutes. I like to use the 70% buttermilk-vegetable oil spread because it tastes so much like butter and has the right moisture content for practically all kinds of baking. You don't know what this spread is? Well, it's actually "I Can't Believe It's Not Butter"—let's call it by its real name. Go to the butter section in the refrigerator case in your supermarket—I'm sure you know where that is.

You'll see lots of products labeled 70% vegetable-oil spread, but only *one* has buttermilk. But again, I'm getting ahead of myself. So where were we? Oh. Then there's monounsaturated fat. This is another fat you find in oils, including canola oil, which is the oil I use in this book. But more about that later.

You may be asking: Why talk about all this? Well, polyunsaturated and monounsaturated fats are thought to help lower your blood cholesterol levels. There's no final word yet as to which may be better, but in any case, either in moderation can only help. Too much cholesterol in your blood, and you may get a waxy buildup on the insides of your blood vessels. Imagine a garden hose that gets a lot of deposit on the inside, and the opening gets narrower and narrower. Get the picture?

SO WHY 30 PERCENT?

When we talk fat, there's one standard we should all understand. The American Heart Association and other similar organizations recommend that you get no more than 30 percent of your total calories from fat. The 30 percent applies to all the food you eat in a day, or even in a week. So you know what that means? You've heard of income averaging? Well, how about fat averaging. If you're honest about it, and that's the key—honesty—you can have dessert. And, that dessert can sometimes sneak above the 30% high-water mark. Just don't get into deep water too often.

Most of the recipes in this book weigh in at 30% calories from fat or less, and some much less. But there are some in the 30% to 35% range, because I snuck in Sacred Fat for better flavor and texture. Then there are even a few beyond that. Life should be more than just constant deprivation. We all need treats, but in moderation.

FLAVOR

You've probably heard me talk about this before. I want to cut fat in my recipes, but I don't want to sacrifice flavor. The bottom line is that if something doesn't taste good, you won't eat it. Right? Especially in desserts, sometimes you need a little extra fat—remember, fat carries flavor—to avoid the cardboard taste that many low-fat desserts have. I call this Sacred Fat—to be used wisely. Sacred Fat is the fat that you or I make a conscious decision to use. And don't sneak around about it. Admit it. Never try to fool yourself. Some of the Sacred Fats I use in desserts are butter (gasp!), chocolate, a sprinkling of ground nuts, and—perish the thought!—even an egg or two on occasion. But where a real egg isn't vital, I'll use a liquid egg substitute if what I really want is the puffing action of the egg white.

Something sweet

Desserts are all about sweetness, and that means calories that come from sugar. A little sugar is okay, and is in fact necessary for a tender cake or cookie.

Also keep in mind that sugar by any other name—molasses, honey, corn syrup, maple syrup, or brown sugar—is still sugar. Once any of them is in your body, they're all the same—no difference. They spell calories. But cooking with different types of sweeteners is something else. You can't just substitute one for the other, since some are liquid and others are solid, and each has its own distinctive chemistry and flavor that will affect the results in very different ways. Whew!—that was a mouthful. Quick! Somebody give me an éclair (page 139)!

When I take you on the grand tour of my kitchen, we'll talk about lots of other ingredients. But for now, let's just focus on sweets—and I'm not talking about me.

Here are the usual sweeteners I keep in my kitchen (and you'll notice there's nothing artificial):

First there's **GRANULATED SUGAR**—that's obvious.

Then, **BROWN SUGAR.** It's a mixture of granulated white sugar and molasses. Dark brown contains more molasses than light brown, and so has a richer flavor. Either one can be substituted measure for measure for white granulated sugar in baking recipes. But take note—the end result will be darker in color and will have a molasses tang. To measure brown sugar, firmly pack it into the measuring cup or spoon.

SUPERFINE SUGAR is more finely ground than regular granulated sugar, so it dissolves instantly. I use it for making meringues. None in the cupboard? Just throw a little granulated sugar in the blender, push the button, and make your own superfine.

CONFECTIONERS' SUGAR is granulated sugar that has been finely ground and mixed with a little cornstarch to prevent caking and crystallization. I use it in icings and frostings because the cornstarch acts as a thickener.

CORN SYRUP is most often used to make candy, as in my lollipops (page 163), because it prevents sugar crystals from forming and keeps the candy mixture smooth. It's also used in baked goods to give them a chewy texture.

HONEY is plant nectar gathered by bees. (We all know that.) A honey can range from pale and delicately flavored, such as clover honey, to dark and deeply flavored buckwheat honey. I personally have never known any bees, but I've known lots of honeys. Substituting honey for sugar in a recipe can be tricky, because honey carries much more flavor. The general rule is to reduce the liquid in the recipe by 3 tablespoons, and then substitute ⅞ cup honey for each cup of sugar.

Let me walk you through my kitchen, open my cupboards, and show you the ingredients I use to make my reduced-fat and reduced-calorie desserts. As we peek here and there, I'll share with you all the things I've learned about lowering the fat in desserts. So put on your walking shoes, because here we go.

all this from a cow?

Remember when life was much simpler? Elsie the cow gave us milk and heavy cream, and that was it. Cows now come in all different shapes and sizes, making lots of reduced-fat and nonfat products.

BUTTERMILK was once made from the liquid left over after butter had been churned. Now—are you ready for this?—it's made by letting bacteria loose (good bacteria, of course, as in yogurt) in regular milk to thicken it and create a tangy taste. There are also low-fat and skim versions. Used in baking, buttermilk makes you think there is fat everywhere. I love to use this in cakes.

EVAPORATED MILK is regular whole milk from which more than half the liquid has been removed by heating. The milk is then homogenized, cooled, poured into cans, and sterilized. What you get is concentrated milk with a consistency similar to heavy cream but without the fat and cholesterol. Good deal. You can use this in some reduced-fat recipes in place of cream. There are also versions made from low-fat milk and skim milk. Do your own taste comparison. Just a spoonful from each can—not the whole can.

SWEETENED CONDENSED MILK is the same as evaporated milk, but with one major difference—sugar! Forty to 45% of this milk mixture is sugar, and we all know what that means—calories. Recently, this has become available in low-fat and fat-free versions. I use the fat-free in *Orange You a Gorgeous Tart!* (page 100) and *Some More S'Mores* (page 49).

YOGURT is nothing more than milk that has been fermented or soured by the action of friendly bacteria. (Here we go with the bacteria again.) The result has a creamy, almost custard-like consistency and a tangy taste. In Middle Eastern countries, words for yogurt translate to mean "life." You remember all those people in Russia who live way beyond 100 because they eat yogurt? Yogurt is high in protein and calcium with lots of minerals such as zinc, phosphorus, and potassium, and B vitamins to boot.

In 1942, a Spanish family introduced Danone yogurt to the United States. Named after Daniel, the son of the company's founder, Danone became Dannon, and you know the rest.

PLAIN YOGURT—the flavored varieties have extra sugar and calories—can be made from whole milk, low-fat milk, or nonfat milk. I like to use yogurt sometimes in baking instead of heavy cream or eggs to create the illusion of fat. Don't forget about frozen yogurt, which can be dolloped on a whole variety of desserts, such as warm apple pie.

Now, let me round up all these dairy products in one place so you can do some comparison shopping. And there are even more new products appearing every day in your supermarket—they're keeping Elsie busy. Make sure to always include paper and pencil on your trips to the market so you can take notes. If the stock boys spot you, just tell them you're from the U.S.D.A., and you're checking freshness labels.

DAIRY PRODUCT	AMOUNT	CALORIES	FAT (GRAMS)
whole milk	1 cup	150	8
2% milk	1 cup	125	5
1% milk	1 cup	110	3
skim milk	1 cup	90	less than ½
heavy cream	1 cup	821	88
light cream	1 cup	698	74
half-and-half	1 cup	315	28
buttermilk (1½%)	1 cup	140	4
low-fat buttermilk	1 cup	110	4
skim buttermilk	1 cup	99	1
evaporated whole milk	1 cup	338	19
low-fat evaporated milk*	1 cup	200	4
evaporated skim milk*	1 cup	199	1
sweetened condensed milk	1 cup	982	27
low-fat sweetened condensed milk	1 cup	960	12
fat-free sweetened condensed milk	1 cup	880	0
sour cream	1 cup	493	48
reduced-fat sour cream	1 cup	360	28
fat-free sour cream	1 cup	150	0
whole-milk yogurt	1 cup	150	8
low-fat plain yogurt	1 cup	144	4
nonfat plain yogurt	1 cup	127	less than ½
cream cheese	2 Tbsp	101	10
neufchâtel cream cheese	2 Tbsp	76	7
50% less-fat cream cheese	2 Tbsp	70	5
fat-free cream cheese	2 Tbsp	50	0

*You may ask why the calories are almost the same for the low-fat and the skim versions. Well, when fat is taken out, something has to go back in to fill up the can. That makes sense, right? It could be more protein, more carbohydrate—but whatever it is, it may add back calories without adding back fat.

better than butter . . .

The 70% buttermilk-vegetable oil spread tastes more like real butter than the other seventy percent spreads in the refrigerator case—it's the buttermilk (and there's no cholesterol here). Remember when we first talked about this on page 13? Go back and take a look. Experiment with all the spreads—don't just take my word for it.

So here are the solid spreads, beginning with the highest in saturated fat:

THE SOLID SPREADS
(FAT GRAMS PER 1 TABLESPOON)

	MONO-UNSATURATED	POLY-UNSATURATED	SATURATED
butter	3.6	0.5	7.6
light butter	N/A	N/A	4.0
vegetable shortening	6.5	1.8	3.9
margarine	5.1	3.6	2.1
70% buttermilk-vegetable oil spread	2.5	2.0	2.0

the good, the bad, and the ugly

In 1966, a large food company (hint: Patton, general—yes, General Foods) gave birth to this NONDAIRY WHIPPED TOPPING (a.k.a. Cool Whip) in a tub. You heard me, tub, not can. This was after the spray can with the dairy topping. If you remember, 1966 was a very busy time—war, protests on college campuses, etc. Housewives across the country were screaming, "Life is becoming too complicated." No one made whipped cream from scratch anymore. Instead, they wanted a ready-to-use, spoonable, low-cost, storable topping that was as good as whipped cream. *Voilà!* Who would have dreamed this was to become America's easiest way to collect food-storage containers. (And don't tell me you haven't used these to store your leftover broccoli or mashed potatoes.) What's in that tub? I'm not going to tell you. Read the label for yourself, but be sure a dictionary is near by. And these days, the topping comes in a reduced-fat and nonfat form as well as the regular. Organize a tasting on your block—just blindfold everyone, and let them go at it, keeping in mind what the alternative is: heavy cream. Save this topping for special occasions, when you want the texture and richness of heavy cream, without all the fat, especially saturated fat.

PER 2 TABLESPOONS	CALORIES	FAT (GRAMS)
extra-creamy nondairy whipped topping	25	2
regular nondairy whipped topping	25	1.5
lite nondairy whipped topping	20	1
fat-free nondairy whipped topping	15	0

oil you need to know

Since we've been talking about butter and other spreads, this is probably the best time to give you the lowdown on how the oils measure up against each other. Here they are, from the highest in monounsaturated fat to the lowest (keep an eye on the saturated fat):

FAT GRAMS IN 1 TABLESPOON

	MONO-UNSATURATED	POLY-UNSATURATED	SATURATED
olive oil	9.9	1.1	1.8
canola oil	8.2	4.1	1
peanut oil	6.2	4.3	2.3
corn oil	3.3	8.0	1.7
safflower oil	1.6	10.1	1.2

CANOLA OIL, as my chart shows, is lower in saturated fat than any other cooking or baking oil. It also contains a lot of those omega-3 fatty acids that made fish famous as brain food and are thought to help lower cholesterol.

I use canola oil in my desserts for its low saturated fat and its mild flavor. But I wouldn't go so far as to say my desserts are brain food.

NONSTICK COOKING SPRAYS have come a long way since that first tall yellow-and-red can. In addition to the standard vegetable-oil spray, there are now specific kinds, such as canola, olive-oil, butter-flavored, and a baking spray that's a mixture of oil and flour. My goodness! With the average vegetable-oil cooking spray, figure about 7 calories per spritz. Use half a spritz, and you're in even better shape.

oh, no! not the (prune) whip!

NATURAL FAT SUBSTITUTES are handy things to know about. Notice I said "natural." I'm an all-natural man—I stay away from the stuff that comes out of the chemistry set. No Dr. Jekyll or Mr. Hyde for me.

APPLESAUCE and **PRUNE PUREE** are probably two of the most popular fat substitutes. They're sweet, so you can use less sugar, and the texture fools you into thinking there's fat in the neighborhood. I use applesauce in my *Keep On Truckin' Brownies* (page 37) and prune puree in my *Walnut–Sour Cream Gems* (page 66).

Prune puree works especially well in dark-colored baked goods, such as a chocolate cake. The prune experts recommend you leave in the recipe at least 1 tablespoon of the fat (butter, butter substitute, margarine, or vegetable oil). You can buy prune "butter" (lekvar) or the new fat-substitute mixtures for baking, made from prunes, apples, and/or plums.

Or, if you really want to do it from scratch, you can make your own prune puree. In a medium saucepan, combine

1 cup pitted prunes with 1 cup water. Cover and bring to a boil. Reduce the heat and simmer until the prunes are soft, about 5 minutes—check with a spoon, not your finger. Place the mixture in a food processor, add another cup of water, and process until smooth. And that's it. You'll have about 1½ cups prune puree. Refrigerate for up to a couple of weeks.

what the chicken doesn't know . . .

The **EGG** is the perfect food—it contains protein, vitamins, and lots of other good things. It adds texture, taste, and richness to desserts. But it also comes with extra baggage—fat and cholesterol. Bad planning on someone's part. So you know us human beings—we can't leave well enough alone. Here's how we've "improved" on Mother Nature:

FAT-FREE LIQUID EGG SUBSTITUTE is now available in refrigerated liquid, frozen, and all kinds of other variations. Read the label, since some are not recommended for baking. In this product, most of the egg yolk, if not all, has been removed, and along with it the fat and cholesterol. What does that leave you with? The white, which is fat-free and cholesterol-free, but with little taste. In most of these products, a little coloring has been added to make it look like the yolks are still there.

THE EGG AND I

	CALORIES	FAT (G)	CHOLESTEROL (MG)
1 egg	75	5	213
¼ cup liquid egg substitute	30	no fat	no cholesterol

POWDERED EGG WHITES are dehydrated egg whites, and are found in the baking aisle, under the brand name "Just Whites." Over the past several years, there have been outbreaks of bacteria-caused food poisoning result-ing from improperly handled eggs and chickens—yes, we do need to talk about this. So for meringues and mousses and other desserts where we've always used beaten uncooked egg whites, this is now a no-no. All dishes with eggs in them need to be cooked to destroy any bacteria (this is not the same friendly bacteria in yogurt and buttermilk). My *Pineapple Dream Boat* (page 170) is a good example of where I use powdered egg whites to make fluffy meringues that aren't cooked.

nutty nutrition

Even though an ounce of most nuts—that's about ¼ cup, give or take a spoonful, depending on the size of the nut—contains about 180 calories and 14 to 19 grams of fat, they're actually good for you. Nuts contain minerals such as copper, magnesium, and potassium, and vita-mins such as E and folic acid. They're also high in polyunsaturated and monounsaturated fatty acids.

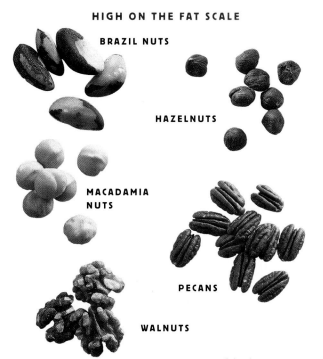

HIGH ON THE FAT SCALE

BRAZIL NUTS

HAZELNUTS

MACADAMIA NUTS

PECANS

WALNUTS

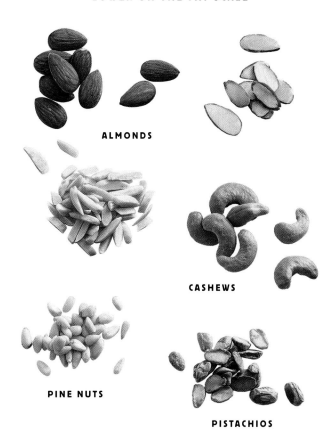

LOWER ON THE FAT SCALE

ALMONDS

PINE NUTS

CASHEWS

PISTACHIOS

And then there's the peanut. It looks like a nut. It feels like a nut. But the common peanut is not a nut at all. It's really the underground seed of a small bush.

PEANUTS

Since nuts do contain fat, they turn rancid after a while. The best way to prevent this is to store them tightly wrapped in the refrigerator for up to 6 months, or in the freezer for up to a year.

chocolate—the brain food

Some of my friends claim that chocolate lifts their spirits and makes them happy. Give me a heaping spoonful of one of my *Some-Like-It-Hot Chocolate Soufflés* (page 136), and I'll smile. But you know, there is a reason for this. Chocolate contains a chemical (phenylethylalamine) that naturally occurs in our brains and is in fact responsible for controlling our moods. But wait a second—does that mean you should stock your cupboards with chocolate candy bars? What do you think?

There's no getting around it. Chocolate, the real stuff, does contain saturated fat. Here's the breakdown for 1 ounce of semisweet chocolate: 9.2 grams saturated fat, 5.2 grams monounsaturated, and 0.5 polyunsaturated. So when you use this stuff, use it wisely.

Here are the chocolates I use, based on 1 ounce:

SEMISWEET CHOCOLATE (148 calories, 16 g fat) is a blend of unsweetened chocolate, cocoa butter, and sugar.

BITTERSWEET CHOCOLATE (135 calories, 11 g fat) has the same ingredients as semisweet but, as you would guess, less sugar.

UNSWEETENED COCOA POWDER (65 calories, 4 g fat) is unsweetened chocolate from which most of the cocoa butter has been removed; the chocolate is then ground and sifted. I use this a lot in my recipes since the calories and fat are so low, and this lets me sneak in a little "real" chocolate for texture and flavor. Oh, if you see Dutch process or European-style cocoa powder, that means it has been treated with an alkali that darkens the cocoa and gives it a distinctive, chocolaty taste.

WHITE CHOCOLATE (151 calories, 9 g fat) is a fake. It's really not chocolate at all—it's cocoa butter mixed with sugar, milk, and vanilla. I like to melt just a little of it and drizzle it over the top of a dessert for a special garnish. Or I grate it on a grater, or shave it with a vegetable peeler. I do try to use it only on desserts—no main courses, breakfast cereals, or mashed potatoes.

softer than a . . .

CAKE FLOUR is more finely milled than regular all-purpose white flour. When it's used in baking, it makes for a more tender cake or cookie. So? This is especially useful in low-calorie and low-fat baking. When you reduce the amount of sugar and/or fat, you usually wind up with something very chewy—save that for chewing gum. (Did I ever tell you about when I had my first stick of gum? Well, maybe I'll tell you later.) So mixing a little cake flour with the all-purpose flour helps to keep things tender.

TO SIFT OR NOT TO SIFT? Sifting used to be important, when we had no machines. It removed foreign objects and large bits of grain. But with today's modern milling practices, you never find any of these things or lumps of flour. But sometimes I do sift. Why? The process incorporates air into the flour—it's called aerating—and this makes for lighter, more tender baked goods. To measure flour, lightly spoon into a measuring cup.

hi! what's your name? justin x. grape

That's a raisin joke, get it? Dried fruits are great add-ins (and good for snacking). They add color and texture as well as little bursts of flavor. Stir them into pudding, cake batter, cookies, or wherever. Here's a rundown on their calories, beginning with the lowest:

CALORIES PER 1/3 CUP DRIED FRUIT

dried apricots	103
dried cranberries	120
dried pineapple	140
raisins	145
dried cherries	160
chopped dates	163
dried blueberries	266

By the way, sometimes a little sugar or oil is used in the processing of dried fruits, so calories may vary from brand to brand.

you've heard of the grapes of wrath?

Well, these are the leaves of pleasure. **PHYLLO,** or filo, dough is used to make those delicate Middle Eastern pastries, both savory and sweet, that have leaves of flaky pastry. I use it in *Have You Athena Baklava?* (page 68) and *Uptown Baked Apple* (page 168). The Greek word *phyllo* in fact means "leaf." Phyllo is sold in rectangular packages of folded-up, tissue-thin layers of dough, frozen or fresh, and generally comes in two sizes, 13 × 9 inches and 17 × 11 inches. For making pastries, the layers are usually spread with melted butter and stacked on top of each other before baking. That's how it get so flaky—the fat. A sheet of phyllo by itself has only 30 calories; it's what you put on it that can make it fattening. Instead of globs of butter, I coat my layers with nonstick cooking spray—such as a butter-flavored spray. (I wish they had a butter-scented room spray or even prime rib scent.) Phyllo dough is fragile and dries out easily, so it's important, while working with it, to keep it covered with waxed paper and a slightly dampened towel.

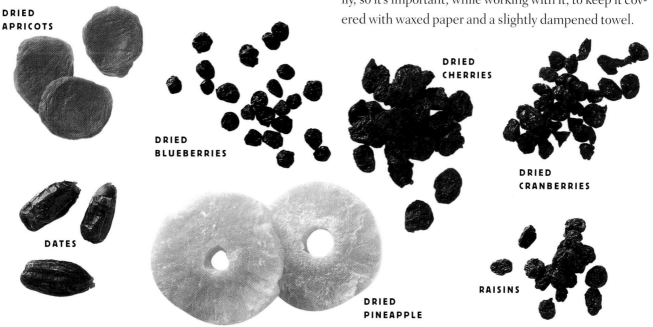

DRIED APRICOTS

DRIED BLUEBERRIES

DRIED CHERRIES

DRIED CRANBERRIES

DATES

DRIED PINEAPPLE

RAISINS

Equipment

This is a list of what you'll need to make all the recipes in my book. I'd assume you're not going to make them all at once—you better not! You probably already have most of this equipment since it's all pretty standard, with the exception of 3 or 4 items. So check out your cupboards and drawers, and make a list. While you're at it, this is probably a good time to get rid of all that stuff that hasn't seen the light of day for a while.

PANS AND DISHES*

8 × 8 × 2-inch square baking pan and dish
9 × 9 × 2-inch square baking pan and dish
13 × 9 × 2-inch baking pan and dish
11 × 7 × 2-inch baking dish
two 9-inch round layer-cake pans
two 8-inch round layer-cake pans
7-inch round layer-cake pan
9-inch springform pan
15 × 10-inch jelly-roll pan
9 × 5 × 3-inch loaf pan
2½-inch muffin-pan cups
Texas-size muffin pan cups
    (3½ × 1¾ inches)
mini muffin pan (gem pan)
10-inch bundt pan
mini bundt pans
mini angel cake pans
9-inch pie pan
9-inch tart pan with removable bottom
1½-quart and 2-quart soufflé dishes

*Sometimes in my recipes I call for a
    nonreactive pan—this means using only a
    metal surface that does not contain aluminum,
    cast iron, or any other material that would react
    with food to change its color and/or taste.

six 6-ounce custard cups or ramekins
six 4-ounce custard cups or ramekins
12-inch pizza pan
baking sheets, preferably nonstick
madeleine pan (see page 32)
saucepans: small, medium, and large, and
    the medium could be nonstick
skillets: small, medium, and large,
    preferably nonstick; plus a 10-inch
    cast-iron skillet

UTENSILS

assortment of mixing bowls
flexible metal spatulas
knives: 8-inch chef's knife,
    small paring knife, long serrated knife,
    long slicing knife
rubber spatulas
whisk
wooden spoons

ELECTRICS

blender
electric mixer
food processor
waffle maker

MEASURING EQUIPMENT

glass measuring cups for liquids
metal measuring cups for dry ingredients
measuring spoons
scale

MISCELLANEOUS

aluminum foil
candy thermometer
assorted cookie cutters
    (2½-inch and ½-inch decorative)
flour sifter
kitchen scissors
kitchen string
oven mitts
parchment paper (especially useful for
    lining baking pans for meringues)
pastry bag with tips (writing, star, etc.)
pastry blender
pastry brush
plastic food-storage bags
plastic wrap
rolling pin
sieve, fine-mesh
waxed paper
wire cooling racks

But wait—I'm not finished yet!

how did these recipes get in this book?

There's a special chapter at the end of the book, "You Can't Take It With You" (the pages are glued together with melted chocolate and peanut butter). Here I've collected six of my all-time favorite outrageous desserts— the ones I must have one last time before I go to that little kitchen in the sky. Make no mistake—these skimp on nothing. But beware, this chapter comes with a warning: Make these recipes only once a year. We're not responsible otherwise.

Tiramisù (page 181)

what's in it? (nutrition breakdown)

Each recipe in this book is followed by a nutrition analysis or breakdown. You certainly won't have a breakdown when you see how little fat is in some of these recipes. I include not only the amount of calories, protein, fat, carbohydrate, sodium, and cholesterol, but also the amount of saturated fat and the percentage of calories from fat. But wait—there's even more! I compare my dessert with the higher-calorie and higher-fat version, so you know where you stand.

pleasure—that's what it's about

Now that you've toured my dessert kitchen and pantry with me, how did you enjoy it? We saw a lot—everything from sugar and chocolate to oils and phyllo. And I've shared with you some of my tips and tricks for keeping a handle on the calorie culprits, fat and sugar.

However as I've said many times before, and this is the most important lesson, but the easiest to remember: Food is our special friend, yours and mine. Treat it as you would any friend—with respect. This is especially important when it comes to desserts. Without blinking an eye, it's easy to take advantage of that friendship with something so sweet—you know what I'm talking about. Approach desserts with good sense, and they will make you smile. They are the icing on the cake of life.

If you are eating healthy food
And moving every day,
You like your work, you like your friends
And make some time for play,

If you have learned to laugh at life
and treasure all its beauty,
And now know when to let things go
Or when to do your duty,

I'd say you've reached that special stage,
No longer just a rookie.
Your elevated title now
Will simply be "Smart Cookie"!

Smart Cookie

Diamond Lemon Bars

MAKES 18 BARS

PREP: 15 MINUTES

BAKE: CRUST AT 350° FOR 13 MINUTES;
BAR AT 350° FOR 30 MINUTES

I have a friend in New York. I can't tell you his name—I just call him the diamond man. He's taught me practically everything I know about diamonds. Did you know diamonds come in purple, tangerine, and red? When I first made this diamond-shaped bar cookie, I said to myself, I'll call the diamond man and tell him, "I've found the most amazing diamond. Let me send it to you and tell me what you think." I did, and he said to me, "Confidentially, Richard, these diamonds are flawless." My advice to you: Keep these in the vault, because you'll be tempted to eat the whole pan.

Nonstick vegetable-oil cooking spray

CRUST

⅔ cup all-purpose flour

⅓ cup graham cracker crumbs

1 tablespoon granulated sugar

3 tablespoons 70% buttermilk-vegetable oil spread

TOPPING

3 large egg whites

1 large whole egg

1 cup granulated sugar

2 tablespoons all-purpose flour

2 teaspoons grated lemon zest

½ cup fresh lemon juice (about 4 lemons)

Confectioners' sugar, for dusting

1 Preheat oven to 350°. Line bottom and sides of 8 × 8 × 2-inch square baking pan with foil, extending foil beyond 2 opposite sides of pan by a few inches. Lightly coat with nonstick cooking spray.

2 *Make crust:* In medium bowl, whisk together flour, graham cracker crumbs, and sugar. Using fingers, rub vegetable oil spread into flour mixture until evenly moistened (you can also use a pastry blender to cut in vegetable oil spread, but it's easier to use your fingers). Crumbs should look like moist sand. Scatter mixture evenly over bottom of prepared pan. Using hands, firmly press mixture into even layer.

Portion control: I had my hand cast in bronze, just to show you how big the diamond should be in relation to a hand. That's it—no bigger.

LIME BARS

Follow directions for lemon bars, substituting 1 teaspoon grated lime zest for the 2 teaspoons lemon zest, and 1½ cups fresh lime juice for the ½ cup lemon juice.

**NUTRIENT VALUE
PER MY BAR**

100 calories, 2 g protein, 2 g fat (21% fat; trace saturated fat), 19 g carbohydrate, 45 mg sodium, 12 mg cholesterol

BAKERY LEMON BAR

143 calories (almost 1½ times the calories), 6 g fat (3 times the fat)

3 Bake in 350° oven until lightly colored, about 13 minutes. Remove from oven, but leave oven on.

4 *Meanwhile, make topping:* In medium bowl, with electric mixer at high speed, beat topping ingredients to combine, about 1 minute. Pour over hot crust. Return to oven and bake until golden brown and almost no indentation remains when lightly

touched in center, about 30 minutes. Transfer pan to wire rack to cool completely.

5 *To serve:* Lift entire square out of pan by foil ends and transfer to cutting board. Cut the square into 3 even strips, and then each strip crosswise, diagonally, into 6 equal diamonds. Dust with confectioners' sugar. These can be refrigerated for a day or two.

Chocolate-Hazelnut Biscotti

MAKES 4½ DOZEN BISCOTTI

PREP: 20 MINUTES

BAKE: AT 350° FOR 24 TO 26 MINUTES;
BAKE SECOND TIME AT 350° FOR
15 MINUTES

All my friends love these crunchy cookies, but not one of them knew how to make them. Well, one did—Judy Pendley. And it's not like they were invented yesterday—they've been around since the 14th century. And guess who invented them? An Italian baker. And in fact, the Italian word *biscotti* means twice baked—that makes them the crunchiest cookie in the world. They love being dunked in milk, hot chocolate, tea, coffee, or as monks once did, in holy wine. But be careful—if you take them to church, don't get caught.

Nonstick vegetable-oil cooking spray
2 cups all-purpose flour
1 cup granulated sugar
⅓ cup unsweetened cocoa powder
1 teaspoon baking soda
½ teaspoon salt
¼ cup mini semisweet chocolate chips
2 large whole eggs
2 large egg whites
2 teaspoons grated orange zest
1 teaspoon pure vanilla or chocolate extract
1 teaspoon instant coffee powder
½ cup hazelnuts, toasted and skinned
   (see Toasty Nuts, page 52)

GLAZE
1 large egg white beaten with 1 teaspoon water

1 Preheat oven to 350°. Lightly coat large baking sheet with cooking spray.

2 In large bowl, whisk together flour, sugar, cocoa powder, baking soda, and salt, until blended. Stir in chocolate chips.

3 In medium bowl, whisk together whole eggs, egg whites, zest, extract, and coffee powder, until powder dissolves. Add to flour mixture along with nuts. With wooden spoon, work wet ingredients into dry ingredients until combined (dough will be sticky).

4 Divide dough in half. With lightly floured hands and on lightly floured surface, roll one half of dough into 14-inch-long rope, then transfer to prepared baking sheet. Flatten rope to 1¾-inch width. Roll remaining dough into another 14-inch-long rope, place 3 to 4 inches away from first rope, and then flatten. Brush ropes with glaze.

5 Bake in 350° oven until firm to the touch, 24 to 26 minutes. Remove from oven and let cool 2 minutes on baking sheet. Leave oven on. Slide loaves onto cutting board. With serrated knife, cut loaves diagonally into ½-inch-thick slices (see photo, page 30). Discard ends. Place slices, cut sides down, back on baking sheet (they can touch).

6 Bake until dry, another 15 minutes, turning biscotti over after 7 minutes. Let cool completely on wire rack. Store in airtight container at room temperature for up to several days.

NUTRIENT VALUE FOR EACH OF MY BISCOTTI

54 calories, 1 g protein,
1 g fat (23% fat; 0 g saturated fat),
9 g carbohydrate, 55 mg sodium,
13 mg cholesterol

TRADITIONAL BISCOTTI

120 calories (more than twice the calories), 5 g fat (5 times the fat)

the secret of twice baked

First, you bake the cookie dough so it looks like a loaf of bread. Then, you cut the loaf diagonally into slices, and back into the oven they go for their crisping (see photo, page 30).

Chocolate-Hazelnut Biscotti and Almond-Ginger Biscotti (page 30)

Almond-Ginger Biscotti

MAKES ABOUT 4½ DOZEN BISCOTTI

PREP: **20** MINUTES

BAKE: AT **350°** FOR **24** TO **26** MINUTES;
BAKE SECOND TIME AT **350°** FOR
15 MINUTES

I love the taste of ginger, especially in gingerbread— but that's powdered ginger. I stumbled across crystallized ginger in the spice section of my supermarket. I had never seen this kind of ginger before. I bought a jar, and on my way to the checkout, I opened it, sniffed, and actually ate the whole thing. So, I went back for another jar. But I was honest—I paid for both. When I got home, I experimented in my kitchen and came up with this version of biscotti, mixing the flavor of the ginger with almonds and vanilla.

Nonstick vegetable-oil cooking spray

2 cups all-purpose flour

1 cup granulated sugar

1 teaspoon baking powder

½ teaspoon salt

½ cup blanched slivered almonds, toasted (see To Toast or Not to Toast, below right)

2 tablespoons crystallized ginger, finely chopped

2 large whole eggs

2 large egg whites

1 teaspoon grated lemon zest

1 teaspoon pure vanilla extract

½ teaspoon almond extract

GLAZE

1 large egg white lightly beaten with 1 teaspoon water

1. Preheat oven to 350°. Lightly coat large baking sheet with nonstick cooking spray.

2. In large bowl, whisk together flour, sugar, baking powder, and salt, until blended. Stir in almonds and ginger.

3. In medium bowl, whisk together whole eggs, egg whites, lemon zest, and extracts. Add to flour mixture. With wooden spoon, work wet ingredients into dry ingredients until combined (dough will be sticky).

4. Divide dough in half. With lightly floured hands and on lightly floured surface, roll one half of dough into 14-inch-long rope, then transfer to prepared baking sheet. Flatten rope to 1¾-inch width. Roll remaining dough into another 14-inch-long rope, place 3 to 4 inches away from first rope, and then flatten. Brush ropes with glaze.

5. Bake in 350° oven until firm to the touch and lightly golden on top, 24 to 26 minutes. Remove from oven and let cool 2 minutes on baking sheet. Leave oven on. Slide loaves onto cutting board. With serrated knife, cut loaves on diagonal into ½-inch-thick slices. Discard ends. Place slices, cut sides down, back on baking sheet (they can touch).

6. Bake until dry, another 15 minutes, turning biscotti over after 7 minutes. Let cool completely on wire racks. Store in airtight container at room temperature for up to several days.

NUTRIENT VALUE FOR EACH OF

MY BISCOTTI

44 calories, 1 g protein, 1 g fat (20% fat; 0 g saturated fat), 8 g carbohydrate, 32 mg sodium, 8 mg cholesterol

TRADITIONAL ALMOND BISCOTTI

86 calories (almost twice the calories), 4 g fat (4 times the fat)

to toast or not to toast

I always vote for toasting—it makes the nuts more flavorful. Spread the almonds out on baking sheet and place in a preheated 350° oven until lightly golden and fragrant, 8 to 10 minutes, stirring occasionally. Keep staring at them very carefully, especially toward the end—there's nothing worse than a burnt nut! As soon as you get even the faintest whiff of toasting, that's it. Immediately dump them onto a paper towel to cool completely before using. If you're toasting a small quantity, toast them in a dry skillet on top of the stove to save turning the oven on.

Madeleine's Cake-Cookies

MAKES 24 LITTLE CAKE-COOKIES

PREP: 20 MINUTES

BAKE: AT 375° FOR 13 TO 15 MINUTES

I have some friends who live at the beach, and they have this beautiful English setter named Madeleine. I asked them once if Madeleine was an old family name. "No—we named her after the cookie in the famous French novel *Remembrance of Things Past.*" The narrator takes a small bite of one of these little cake-cookies, and it's love at first taste. There's a bakery in L.A. that makes wonderful madeleines. Even if you just lightly touch them, the butter oozes out. Mine are much more sensible—still the great taste, but with much less butter.

2 tablespoons unsalted butter, melted
Cake flour, for dusting pan
2 large eggs, separated
⅛ teaspoon salt
½ cup granulated sugar
1 tablespoon canola oil
2 teaspoons grated lemon zest
2 teaspoons fresh lemon juice
¼ teaspoon lemon extract
⅓ cup + 1 tablespoon <u>sifted</u> cake flour
Confectioners' sugar, for dusting

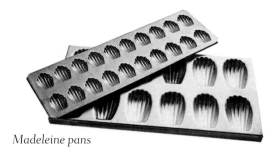

Madeleine pans

1 Preheat oven to 375°. Brush 24 madeleine molds or mini-muffin pan-cups (or work in batches with as many pans as you have) with 1 tablespoon melted butter. Dust molds lightly with a little cake flour, tapping out excess.

2 In medium bowl, with electric mixer on medium speed, beat together egg whites and salt until soft peaks form. Beat in 3 tablespoons granulated sugar until whites form stiff and glossy peaks.

3 In second medium bowl, combine egg yolks, remaining 1 tablespoon melted butter, and remaining 5 tablespoons sugar. With mixer on medium speed, beat until light and fluffy, about 2 minutes. Add oil, lemon zest, lemon juice, and lemon extract and beat until creamy, about 1 minute. Reduce mixer speed to low and beat in flour just until combined.

4 Fold about one-quarter of whites into yolk mixture. Fold in remaining whites just until combined. Drop 1 tablespoon of batter into each prepared mold.

5 Bake in 375° oven until golden around edges and tops spring back when lightly touched, 13 to 15 minutes. Cool madeleines in molds on wire rack for 2 minutes. Loosen edges with paring knife and remove cakes from molds to racks to cool completely. Dust with confectioners' sugar. Serve.

NUTRIENT VALUE PER MY MADELEINE

43 calories, 1 g protein, 2 g fat (41% fat; 1 g saturated fat), 6 g carbohydrate, 17 mg sodium, 20 mg cholesterol

THE CLASSIC MADELEINE

170 calories (4 times the calories), 10 g fat (5 times the fat)

got to have butter!

This is one of those instances where you have to have a little butter. Greasing the pans with that lovely golden fat makes the outside of the madeleines buttery golden and slightly crisp. But I've replaced the butter in the madeleines themselves with oil, and used less sugar. These are best eaten soon after they come out of the oven.

Sealed with a Kiss

MAKES ABOUT 52 VANILLA-ALMOND KISSES

PREP: 30 MINUTES

BAKE: AT 225° FOR 1¼ TO 1½ HOURS

I come from a family where there was always a lot of kissing. I'm a kisser from way back. And even now, with my career and all my traveling, that's practically all I do. I have probably kissed more people than the Pope. If you multiply 100 shopping-mall visits a year, at 10,000 kisses per mall—you have 1,000,000 kisses right there! That's why I go through so many cases of chapstick in a year. I've planted smooches on millions and millions of people, all over the world, and they've all been fat-free. So now, I've created for you these special, fat-free pastel kisses you can have even when I'm not around, in remembrance of *moi*.

¼ cup + ½ cup superfine sugar

1½ tablespoons cornstarch

3 large egg whites, at room temperature

¼ teaspoon cream of tartar

1 teaspoon pure vanilla extract

½ teaspoon almond extract

1 Preheat oven to 225°. Line large baking sheet with parchment paper, or use reusable nonstick cookie sheet liner. Place a ⅜-inch-wide star tip into 12-inch pastry bag. (If you don't have pastry bag and star tip, don't worry! You can drop little mounds of meringue with a measuring tablespoon—they won't look as pretty as the piped ones, but they'll taste just as good.)

2 In small bowl, mix ¼ cup sugar with cornstarch and reserve. In medium bowl, with electric mixer on high speed, beat together egg whites and cream of tartar until soft peaks form. Gradually beat in remaining ½ cup sugar, 1 tablespoon at a time. Reduce mixer speed to medium and gradually beat in reserved sugar-cornstarch mixture until incorporated. Add vanilla and almond extracts. Increase mixer speed to high and beat 5 minutes, scraping down sides of bowl several times, until stiff and glossy peaks form. If using the pastry bag, fill with mixture.

3 Onto prepared baking sheet, pipe kisses, spacing ½ inch apart. Or drop mixture by rounded table-spoonfuls.

4 For crisp meringues, bake in 225° oven until firm to the touch and crisp throughout, about 1½ hours, turning baking sheet once from front to back halfway through baking. For chewier meringues, bake about 1¼ hours, rotating sheet once halfway through baking. Cool meringues slightly on baking sheet on wire rack. Transfer meringues to wire rack to cool completely. Store in airtight container at room temperature for up to 3 days.

NUTRIENT VALUE PER MY KISS

13 calories, 0 g protein, 0 g fat (0% fat; 0 g saturated fat), 3 g carbohydrate, 3 mg sodium, 0 mg cholesterol

A TRADITIONAL KISS

31 calories (more than twice the calories). Some meringue cookies on the market contain 1 gram of fat. But you won't be buying them anymore—you'll be making these.

kiss variations

ORANGE KISSES: Follow directions for vanilla-almond kisses with following changes: Substitute 1 teaspoon orange extract for vanilla and almond extracts and add 12 drops orange food coloring. Bake as directed. Makes about 52 kisses.

STRAWBERRY KISSES: Follow directions for vanilla-almond kisses with following changes: Substitute 1½ teaspoons strawberry extract for vanilla and almond extracts and add 12 drops red food coloring. Bake as directed. Makes about 52 kisses.

MINT KISSES: Follow directions for vanilla-almond kisses with following changes: Substitute ¼ teaspoon mint extract for almond extract and add 12 drops green food coloring. Bake as directed. Makes about 52 kisses.

COCOA KISSES: Follow directions for vanilla-almond kisses with following changes: Substitute 1½ teaspoons chocolate extract for vanilla and almond extracts. After beating egg white mixture, sift 2 tablespoons unsweetened cocoa powder over mixture and fold it gently in until thoroughly blended. Bake as directed. Makes about 52 kisses.

WHAT TASTES LIKE FAT, AND FEELS LIKE FAT? APPLESAUCE!

This is a baker's trick, substituting applesauce for most of the butter or other fat. The texture of applesauce in baked desserts fools your tongue—it thinks it's wrapped itself around tasty globs of fat. Plus, applesauce adds a touch of natural sweetness, so you can cut back on the sugar.

nuts: the sacred fat

Know why nuts taste go good? Fat! I use a very small amount in these brownies for their delicious flavor. But if you want to eliminate another gram of fat per brownie, just leave out the peanuts. I know, I know— peanuts are not nuts, but they sure look and taste like them.

Keep On Truckin' Brownies

MAKES 12 BROWNIES

PREP: 15 MINUTES

BAKE: AT 375° FOR 25 TO 28 MINUTES

I first tasted Rocky Road ice cream at Baskin Robbins in the '70s—it was flavor 23. I remember racing into the store around the corner from where I lived when I saw the new flavor sign go up in the window. "Three scoops, please," I whispered. I separated the little marshmallows into the right side of my mouth, the chocolate chips in the center, and the peanuts into the left side—I looked like a chipmunk! I loved this so much, I ate enough that first time to make me weigh almost as much as a small pickup truck. This brownie is my re-creation of that Rocky Road flavor.

Nonstick vegetable-oil cooking spray

¼ cup canola oil

¾ cup granulated sugar

½ cup packed light-brown sugar

1 large egg

½ cup unsweetened applesauce

½ teaspoon pure vanilla extract

⅓ cup unsweetened cocoa powder

1 cup all-purpose flour

¼ teaspoon salt

¼ teaspoon baking powder

¼ cup semisweet chocolate chips

1 cup mini-marshmallows

3 tablespoons chopped peanuts

1 Preheat oven to 375°. Lightly coat 8 × 8 × 2-inch square baking pan with nonstick cooking spray.

2 In medium bowl, whisk together oil, both sugars, egg, applesauce, and vanilla, until blended. Whisk in cocoa powder until blended. Stir in flour, salt, and baking powder, until combined. Scrape into prepared pan.

3 Bake in 375° oven for 20 minutes. Remove pan from oven and sprinkle evenly with chocolate chips, then marshmallows and peanuts. Return to oven and bake until marshmallows are lightly golden, and small knife inserted in center of brownie comes out clean, another 5 to 8 minutes. Cool in pan on wire rack. Cut into 12 brownies.

NUTRIENT VALUE PER MY BROWNIE

211 calories, 3 g protein, 8 g fat (34% fat; 1 g saturated fat), 35 g carbohydrate, 66 mg sodium, 18 mg cholesterol

THE USUAL ROCKY ROAD BROWNIE

300 calories (almost 1½ times the calories), 20 g fat (2½ times the fat)

the marshmallow plant

You're not going to believe this, but marshmallows once actually came from a plant. No, they weren't the buds. The flavoring for marshmallows came from an extract made from the root of a perennial herb. Modern marshmallows are made from corn syrup, gelatin, and gum arabic, a natural thickener made from tree bark. So, we went from an herb to a tree, but I still wouldn't go so far as to call marshmallows organic! No fat in them, but watch out for the calories from the sugar in the corn syrup.

I-Thought-It-Was-a-Hot-Dog Cannoli Cookie

MAKES 15 COOKIE CANNOLIS

PREP: 30 MINUTES

BAKE: AT 375° FOR 5 TO 6 MINUTES

PER BATCH

I had my first cannoli ever in Pisa. I went directly from the airport to the famous leaning tower. And there at the base of the tower was, not an espresso bar, but a cannoli stand! Now from a distance I thought it was a hot-dog stand—you know, kosher . . . I didn't know what a cannoli was. I thought it was a Dean Martin song. So I walked over, singing, "Ca-a-a-annoli, ca-a-a-annoli, whoooah, whoooah . . . " And here were all these Italian women, piping a cheesy filling into tubes of pastry, and then dipping the ends into chopped pistachios. It's not a hot dog, I thought, but it can't be all that bad. It's a very long walk to the top of the tower, and I didn't want to get hungry, so I bought a couple for the climb. And that's why the tower is now closed. Too many people walked to the top carrying cannolis, and the tower leaned over even more.

This is my version, done as a cookie, and much smaller. Talk about portion control—these are cocktail-size.

Nonstick vegetable-oil cooking spray

CANNOLI COOKIES

2 large egg whites

⅓ cup packed light-brown sugar

1 tablespoon canola oil

1 tablespoon 70% buttermilk-vegetable oil spread, melted

½ teaspoon pure vanilla extract

⅓ cup + 1 tablespoon all-purpose flour

FILLING

½ cup part-skim ricotta cheese

3 tablespoons nonfat cream cheese, at room temperature

3 tablespoons confectioners' sugar

1 teaspoon pure vanilla extract

¾ teaspoon grated orange zest

Pinch ground nutmeg

½ cup frozen reduced-fat nondairy whipped topping, thawed

1½ tablespoons semisweet mini-chocolate chips

1. Preheat oven to 375°. Lightly coat baking sheet with nonstick cooking spray.

2. *Make cookies:* In medium bowl, whisk together egg whites, sugar, oil, vegetable oil spread, and vanilla, until sugar dissolves. Whisk in flour until smooth. Onto prepared baking sheet, spoon 3 mounds, using 2 teaspoons of batter for each, spacing mounds about 4 inches apart. With back of spoon, spread each mound into 3½-inch round.

3. Bake in 375° oven just until turning golden around edges, 5 to 6 minutes. Using a metal spatula, immediately loosen 1 cookie from sheet and shape into tube form. Place cookie tube, seam side down, on

THERE'S A PLACE AND A TIME

I love cream cheese. I've used it all my life—I just love opening the silver wrapper. Now, there's a nonfat cream cheese. I use a little in this dessert to add creaminess to the ricotta filling, and it works really well with the strongly flavored vanilla extract and grated orange zest. So try it.

NUTRIENT VALUE PER MY CANNOLI COOKIE

71 calories, 2 g protein, 3 g fat (38% fat; 1 g saturated fat), 9 g carbohydrate, 41 mg sodium, 3 mg cholesterol

GROWN-UP CANNOLI

580 calories (more than 8 times the calories), 33 g fat (11 times the fat)

work surface and let cool completely. Repeat with remaining 2 cookies on sheet. Repeat with remaining batter, cooling and wiping a baking sheet previously used, and recoating with cooking spray. Cookies can be stored in airtight container for up to 3 days. If necessary, cookies can be recrisped in a 300° oven for 3 minutes.

4 *Make filling:* In medium bowl, with electric mixer on medium speed, beat together ricotta, cream cheese, confectioners' sugar, vanilla, orange zest, and nutmeg. Fold in whipped topping and chocolate chips. Spoon into pastry bag fitted with wide round tip, or into small plastic food-storage bag with ½ inch of corner snipped off. Pipe filling into cookie cannoli shells. Serve immediately.

Mama Mia! A Brownie Pizza!

MAKES 12 SERVINGS

PREP: 25 MINUTES

BAKE: AT 350° FOR 10 MINUTES

Does this sound familiar? "Yes . . . I'll hold. Yes . . . there's six of us (well, really only two). Do you have the deep dish? Can you send an extra-large deep dish? Can you put extra cheese on it? Can it be here in 30 minutes?" How many times have we all had this telephone conversation—it's a ritual. Now there's Thai pizza, ham-and-cheese pizza. But I've created a dessert pizza. It'll fool your eyes without putting treadmarks on your thighs!

Nonstick vegetable-oil cooking spray

BROWNIE BASE

½ cup packed light-brown sugar

½ cup coarsely chopped pitted dates

⅓ cup liquid fat-free egg substitute, thawed if frozen

3 tablespoons canola oil

3 tablespoons low-fat buttermilk

¾ teaspoon pure vanilla extract

⅔ cup cake flour

¼ cup unsweetened cocoa powder

¼ teaspoon baking soda

¼ teaspoon salt

PIZZA TOPPING

12 medium to large fresh strawberries, hulled

¼ cup strawberry jam

4 ounces fresh pineapple, cut into ¼-inch-thick wedges

2 kiwifruit, peeled and cut into ¼-inch-thick slices

12 large blackberries

2 ounces white chocolate

1 Preheat oven to 350°. Lightly coat 12-inch pizza pan with nonstick cooking spray.

2 *Make brownie base:* In food processor, combine brown sugar and dates. Process until dates are finely chopped. Add egg substitute, oil, buttermilk, and vanilla, and pulse on/off several times to blend. Add flour, cocoa powder, baking soda, and salt, and pulse 2 or 3 times just until flour is moistened; do not overmix. Pour batter into prepared pan and spread evenly.

3 Bake in 350° oven until set and dry to touch, about 10 minutes. Cool brownie base in pan on wire rack.

4 *Make pizza topping:* Thinly slice 10 strawberries. In food processor, combine remaining 2 strawberries and jam, and puree. Spread puree over brownie base, leaving ½-inch border all around edge. Arrange strawberry slices, pineapple slices, kiwifruit slices, and blackberries on top.

5 Grate white chocolate on medium-coarse grater and sprinkle over pizza. Now doesn't that look like mozzarella cheese?

NUTRIENT VALUE PER SERVING OF MY DESSERT PIZZA

167 calories, 3 g protein, 6 g fat (30% fat; 2 g saturated fat), 28 g carbohydrate, 102 mg sodium, 1 mg cholesterol

TRADITIONAL PIZZA

510 calories (3 times the calories), 21 g fat (3½ times the fat)

To Linzer, with Love

MAKES ABOUT 2 DOZEN SANDWICH COOKIES
(PLUS TINY COOKIE CUTOUTS)

PREP: 30 MINUTES, PLUS CHILLING
BAKE: AT 350° FOR 7 TO 10 MINUTES
PER BATCH

In Linz, Austria, there a was a baker named Herr Linzer. He loved his wife so much. On their anniversary, he asked her, "Heidi, do you want diamonds, emeralds, or rubies?" She said, "No. I want you to create a very special cookie for me." Into the kitchen he went, and two days later he came out with the most beautiful spice cookie. He named it after her. No, not the Heidi cookie—the Linzer cookie. He loved her more than any star in the sky, and with all his heart—that's why he made these loving shapes.

2 cups cake flour
1 teaspoon baking powder
¾ teaspoon ground cinnamon
¼ teaspoon salt
3 tablespoons unsalted butter, at room temperature
2 tablespoons canola oil
¾ cup granulated sugar
1 teaspoon grated lemon zest
1 large egg
1 teaspoon pure vanilla extract
Nonstick vegetable-oil cooking spray
¼ cup sliced blanched almonds, chopped
⅓ cup seedless raspberry jam
Confectioners' sugar, for dusting (optional)

1 In medium bowl, stir together flour, baking powder, cinnamon, and salt.

2 In second medium bowl, with electric mixer on medium speed, beat butter until smooth. Beat in oil until well blended. Beat in granulated sugar and lemon zest, until light. Beat in egg and vanilla. Reduce mixer speed to low and beat in flour mixture to make soft dough. Divide dough in half, shape each into a disk, wrap in plastic, and place in freezer until firm, about 20 minutes.

3 Preheat oven to 350°. Lightly coat baking sheets with nonstick cooking spray.

4 Roll half the dough out between 2 sheets of waxed paper to ⅛-inch thickness. Remove top sheet of waxed paper. Using 2½-inch decorative cookie cutter, cut out cookies. With floured metal spatula, transfer cookies to prepared baking sheet, spacing 1 inch apart. Reserve scraps. Using ½-inch decorative cutter, cut out centers from half the cookies (leaving the others whole). Remove dough centers with tip of knife and place beside cookies on

prepared baking sheet. Repeat with remaining dough. Reroll scraps and cut out more cookies. Sprinkle half the cookies (only ones with centers cut out) with almonds.

5 Bake solid cookies, cutout cookies, and tiny cutout centers in 350° oven until lightly browned around edges, 7 to 10 minutes (cutout centers will bake slightly faster than the other cookies). Transfer cookies and cutout centers to wire racks to cool completely. Cookies can be stored in airtight container at room temperature for up to 2 or 3 days.

6 Just before serving, spread jam over solid cookies, and top each one with a cutout cookie to make a "sandwich." If desired, dust lightly with confectioners' sugar. Use the tiny cutouts for wise snacking.

NUTRIENT VALUE PER MY SANDWICH COOKIE

97 calories, 1 g protein, 3 g fat (30% fat; 1 g saturated fat), 16 g carbohydrate, 43 mg sodium, 13 mg cholesterol

THE CLASSIC LINZER TART

340 calories (3½ times the calories), 18 g fat (6 times the fat)

herr linzer appliqués

Try this variation: Make small cutouts in only one-third of the cookies. Spread jam on all the solid cookies. On half of those, place a small cutout center in the middle; this will reduce the amount of fat and calories per cookie. On the other half of the solid cookies, place a cutout cookie.

Bogging for Oatmeal-Cranberry Cookies

MAKES ABOUT 4 DOZEN COOKIES

PREP: 20 MINUTES

BAKE: AT 350° FOR 10 TO 12 MINUTES

One autumn a few years ago, when I was visiting a mall in Massachusetts, some friends said, "Let us take you to the bogs." I said, "Sure." But really, I had absolutely no idea what a bog was. Off we went to Cape Cod, along Route 125, the "Cranberry Highway." We were going to the cranberry bogs. Ohhh. I put on a special wet suit, got my cranberry rake, and into the bog I went to gather those crimson jewels. Now that I've bogged, I just can't understand why people go bungee jumping. When the jumping's over, what do you have left? Bruises and messed-up hair. With bogging, you can make cranberry cookies.

Nonstick vegetable-oil cooking spray
1 cup all-purpose flour
½ teaspoon baking soda
¼ teaspoon salt
½ cup (1 stick) 70% buttermilk-vegetable oil spread, at room temperature
⅔ cup packed light-brown sugar
2 large egg whites
1 teaspoon pure vanilla extract
1⅓ cups dried cranberries
1 cup old-fashioned rolled oats

1 Preheat oven to 350°. Lightly coat baking sheets with nonstick cooking spray.

2 In medium bowl, stir together flour, baking soda, and salt.

3 In second medium bowl, with electric mixer on medium speed, beat vegetable oil spread until smooth and creamy, 1 to 2 minutes. Beat in brown sugar until light and fluffy, 2 to 3 minutes. Beat in egg whites, one at a time, until well combined. Beat in vanilla. Add flour mixture and stir by hand until flour is no longer visible. Stir in cranberries and oats.

4 Onto prepared baking sheets, drop batter by slightly rounded teaspoons, spacing them 1½ inches apart.

5 Bake in 350° oven until light golden brown, 10 to 12 minutes. Remove to a wire rack to cool. Cookies can be stored in airtight container for up to 2 days.

NUTRIENT VALUE PER MY COOKIE

50 calories, 1 g protein, 2 g fat (32% fat; 0 g saturated fat), 8 g carbohydrate, 43 mg sodium, 0 mg cholesterol

TRADITIONAL OATMEAL COOKIE

117 calories (1⅔ times the calories), 4 g fat (twice the fat)

Minneappleis Streusel Bar Cookies

MAKES 16 BARS

PREP: 20 MINUTES

BAKE: OATS AT 350° FOR 8 MINUTES;

DOUGH BASE AT 350° FOR 10 MINUTES;

THEN WITH TOPPING FOR 30 MINUTES

Believe it or not, I have picked apples. A lot of people can't say that. They've picked them at the supermarket. I'm talking about going to a huge apple farm outside Minneapolis, and getting up on a ladder. Yes, me! When I finished picking, this lovely apple-cheeked woman (her name tag read, "Joan—I love apples, too") came up to me and said, "Follow me into my kitchen—I'm going to make something very special for you." Joan threw together an apple streusel. So that's what a streusel is. When I returned to my own kitchen at home, this is what I made.

Nonstick vegetable-oil cooking spray

DOUGH

½ cup old-fashioned rolled oats

⅔ cup all-purpose flour

3 tablespoons granulated sugar

3 tablespoons 70% buttermilk-vegetable oil spread, chilled

TOPPING

2 sweet apples (12 ounces), such as Golden Delicious, Rome, or McIntosh, peeled, cored, each cut lengthwise into eighths, and thinly sliced crosswise (2 cups)

2 tablespoons fresh lemon juice

⅓ cup all-purpose flour

¼ cup granulated sugar

¼ teaspoon ground cinnamon

2 tablespoons 70% buttermilk-vegetable oil spread, chilled

1 Preheat oven to 350°. Line 8 × 8 × 2-inch square baking pan with aluminum foil, leaving 2-inch overhang around all sides. Lightly coat with nonstick cooking spray.

2 *Make dough:* On baking sheet, spread oats in even layer.

3 Bake in 350° oven until lightly toasted and crisp, about 8 minutes. Leave oven on.

4 In food processor, combine oats and flour. Process until oats are coarsely ground. Transfer to medium bowl. Stir in sugar. With fingertips, rub in vegetable oil spread until mixture resembles coarse crumbs. Press dough evenly over bottom of prepared pan.

5 Bake in 350° oven until lightly colored, about 10 minutes.

6 *Meanwhile, make topping:* In medium bowl, toss apples with lemon juice. In separate bowl, stir together flour, sugar, and cinnamon. With fingertips, work in vegetable oil spread until mixture resembles coarse meal. Spoon apples over top of baked dough. Scatter flour mixture evenly over apples.

WHAT'S A STREUSEL? WILL IT MAKE MY HAIR CURLY?

The word *streusel*, in German, means "sprinkle" or "strew." I suppose you could sprinkle this in your hair, but it might attract bears since it's a mixture of sugar, flour, butter, and a variety of spices. Where it really belongs is sprinkled over coffeecakes, breads, or, in this case, cookies.

7 Bake in 350° oven until topping is lightly crisped and apples are tender, about 30 minutes. Transfer pan to wire rack and cool for 5 minutes. Using foil overhang as handles, lift entire square out of pan. Cool slightly. Cut into 16 bars. Serve warm. Or store, covered, in the refrigerator for up to 2 days.

NUTRIENT VALUE PER MY STREUSEL BAR
98 calories, 1 g protein, 3 g fat (31% fat; 1 g saturated fat), 16 g carbohydrate, 30 mg sodium, 0 mg cholesterol
TRADITIONAL STREUSEL BAR
133 calories (1⅓ times the calories), 6 g fat (twice the fat)

Some More S'Mores

MAKES 6 SANDWICH COOKIES

PREP: 15 MINUTES

One summer my parents sent my brother Lenny to camp in Stony Lake, Michigan. He loved it. So they decided, even though I was terrified of anything with the word "camp" in it, that I should go, too. The boys' barracks were 5 miles from the dining hall, which was right next door to the girls' cabins. So, I had to walk 5 miles for every meal, including breakfast. The girls were never allowed in the boys' barracks, and vice versa. But one night, I snuck from the dining hall down to the beach. There were the girls, all gathered around a campfire. It was like an Anne Rice novel. I was spellbound. I'm from New Orleans, Louisana, where we never build campfires. The girls were unwrapping things and laughing. I crept closer and closer, and finally they saw me and invited me over. And that's when I had my first s'more. It was like the Dead Poets Society in the woods, but with chocolate. I went back for many more nighttime s'more visits. All that gooey chocolate dripped down on my shirt, and the stains never came out. So I always wore that same shirt—it was my s'more shirt.

¼ cup semisweet chocolate chips

3 tablespoons fat-free sweetened condensed milk

1 tablespoon unsweetened cocoa powder

1 tablespoon confectioners' sugar

6 whole graham cracker rectangles, split in half to make 12 squares

6 tablespoons marshmallow creme

1 In small saucepan, heat chips and condensed milk over low heat, stirring until smooth. Remove from heat. Stir in cocoa and sugar until smooth. (If mixture is made ahead, reheat in microwave at 30% power until good spreading consistency, 1 minute.)

2 On each of 6 graham cracker squares, spread 1 tablespoon of chocolate mixture. On each of 6 remaining squares, spread 1 tablespoon of marshmallow creme. Sandwich both halves together for all 6 and serve warm or at room temperature.

NUTRIENT VALUE PER MY S'MORE

187 calories, 2 g protein, 4 g fat (19% fat; 2 g saturated fat), 38 g carbohydrate, 107 mg sodium, 0 mg cholesterol

THE ORIGINAL S'MORE FROM CAMP

234 calories (1¼ times the calories), 11 g fat (almost 3 times the fat)

GRAHAM CRACKERS FROM HEAVEN

Ready for this one? A Presbyterian minister named Sylvester Graham invented these crackers in the 1800s. Really! He was against white flour or any processed food that deviated from its natural state. "Keep it pure! Keep it pure!" he shouted to his followers. So he invented graham flour made from crushed wheat. What would Sylvester think of today's chocolate-flavored graham crackers? Sinful!

Seek Your Fortune, Cookie

MAKES ABOUT 16 COOKIES

PREP: 30 MINUTES

BAKE: AT 350° FOR 5 MINUTES PER BATCH

We all know fortune cookies came from China. Wrong! They were created in California in the early 1900s. Some say a Chinese immigrant in an L.A. bakery made these cookies and filled them with inspirational messages to uplift the spirits of the homeless. But San Franciscans say a Japanese caretaker for a local tea garden put thank you notes in these cookies.

Well, in any event, I had a favorite Chinese restaurant in L.A. I used to love to go to for spring rolls. But recently, the fortunes in their fortune cookies started to get me a little depressed. I didn't need to read things like: "You will lose your hair," "You will gain 50 pounds," or "Cookbooks will no longer be popular." So I decided to make my own fortune cookies with my own fortunes. "You will sell lots of books and videos," "You will be voted one of the best-dressed men of the decade," and "Saturated fat will be discovered to prolong life."

- 3 tablespoons light-brown sugar
- ¼ cup granulated sugar
- 2 large egg whites
- 2 tablespoons canola oil
- ¼ teaspoon pure vanilla extract
- ¼ teaspoon almond extract
- 2 drops yellow food coloring (optional)
- ⅓ cup + 1 tablespoon all-purpose flour
- Nonstick vegetable-oil cooking spray
- 24 paper fortune strips (2¼ × ½ inch), with fortunes

1. In medium bowl, press brown sugar with back of spoon to remove all lumps. Add granulated sugar, egg whites, oil, vanilla and almond extracts, and food coloring, if using, and whisk until blended. Sift in flour and whisk until smooth. Let batter stand for 20 minutes.

2. Meanwhile, preheat oven to 350°. Lightly coat baking sheet with nonstick cooking spray. Spoon 1 measuring tablespoon of batter onto prepared baking sheet. With back of spoon, spread batter to 3-inch circle with even thickness. Repeat 3 more times on sheet. Place a muffin pan nearby.

3. Bake in 350° oven until golden around edges, about 5 minutes. Coat spatula with nonstick cooking spray and loosen cookies immediately from sheet. Remove 1 cookie to work surface. (Return baking sheet with remaining cookies to oven to keep them soft, keeping oven door open.) Flip one cookie over, lay fortune paper in center, and fold cookie in half over fortune. Fold cookie in half again, bending on straight side, to form traditional fortune-cookie shape. Place in muffin-pan cup to hold shape and cool. Repeat with remaining 3 cookies.

Leave room for dessert, sweetie pie.

A BETTER FORTUNE

As you know, commercially prepared fortune cookies taste like cardboard. So, this is one of those occasions where the only way to make something better is to sneak in a little fat. And that's what I did by adding canola oil. This fat is okay—it's mostly all monounsaturated with hardly any saturated.

KEEP THE FORTUNE CRISPY

Humidity will affect the crispness of these cookies. If they become slightly soggy, recrisp them in a 275° oven for about 10 minutes. When making these, make sure you have a muffin pan nearby for holding the cookies while they cool.

4 Cool baking sheet, wipe clean, and coat with cooking spray. Repeat with remaining batter and fortune papers. Store cooled cookies in airtight container at room temperature for up to 1 week.

NUTRIENT VALUE PER MY FORTUNE COOKIE
47 calories, 1 g protein, 2 g fat (33% fat; 0 g saturated fat), 7 g carbohydrate, 8 mg sodium, 0 mg cholesterol
COMMERCIAL FORTUNE COOKIE IS ABOUT THE SAME, BUT DOESN'T TASTE AS GOOD

toasty nuts

Toasting hazelnuts, a.k.a. filberts, deepens their flavor and makes it easier to remove the bitter-tasting skins. Spread the nuts out in a jelly-roll pan or other baking pan with sides—you don't want to be down on your hands and knees searching in the bottom of the oven for loose nuts. Put the pan in a preheated 350° oven, stirring the nuts occasionally, until they smell nutty and are lightly colored, 6 to 8 minutes. While still warm, place the nuts in a clean kitchen towel and rub them to remove the skins, just as if you were drying your hair. To grind them, wait until they are totally cool. Then in a food processor, grind them with on/off pulses. Don't overgrind, or you'll be spreading nut butter on your cookies!

"I Do, I Do" Wedding Cookies

MAKES ABOUT 2 DOZEN COOKIES

PREP: 20 MINUTES

BAKE: AT 400° FOR 15 TO 20 MINUTES

The reason I like to go to weddings is that I love the receptions. I can't wait until the exchange of vows, so I can eat. When I was growing up in New Orleans, the first thing I would do every Saturday morning is get the newspaper and turn immediately to the society page to check out the lineup of weddings for the day. "Angelina Filé and Antoine Andouille are getting married today at the St. Louis Cathedral in New Orleans, and the wedding reception will be at Commander's Palace." That's it! I'd put on my little suit, grab my change, and take a streetcar, not named Desire, to the reception. People would ask if I were a friend of the bride or the groom. I'd smile and say yes. Of all the things on the buffet table, the wedding cookies were always my most favorite. You'd see lots of people walking around with powdered-sugar moustaches, and this was long before the milk commercials.

½ cup (1 stick) light butter, at room temperature

¼ cup confectioners' sugar

1 teaspoon pure vanilla extract

1 cup cake flour

Large pinch salt

¼ cup hazelnuts, toasted, skinned, and ground
   (see Toasty Nuts, opposite page)

Additional confectioners' sugar, for coating
   (about ½ cup)

1 Preheat oven to 400°.

2 In medium bowl, with electric mixer on medium speed, beat together butter and confectioners' sugar until smooth and creamy. Beat in vanilla. Reduce mixer speed to low and beat in flour and salt. Beat in hazelnuts. Roll into 1-inch balls. (If dough is very soft, refrigerate 20 to 30 minutes.) Place on ungreased baking sheet, spacing 1½ inches apart.

3 Bake in 400° oven until pale golden, 15 to 20 minutes.

4 While still hot, roll cookies in confectioners' sugar to coat. Cool completely. Roll again in confectioners' sugar. Cookies can be stored in airtight container at room temperature for up to 2 days.

NUTRIENT VALUE PER MY COOKIE

68 calories, 1 g protein, 4 g fat (56% fat; 1 g saturated fat), 7 g carbohydrate, 48 mg sodium, 0 mg cholesterol

TRADITIONAL WEDDING COOKIE

87 calories (1¼ times the calories), 6 g fat (1½ times the fat)

why light butter?

I've used light butter in this recipe for the flavor, so I'm saving some calories and fat. The 70% buttermilk-vegetable oil spread I usually use doesn't work here because its moisture content would make the cookies soggy rather than melt-in-your-mouth. The percentage of calories from fat is high, and that's because the calories are really low. But this is a nut cookie, and there's no getting around that. There's a reason why they melt in your mouth. So—for celebrations only!

You may s-t-r-o-l-l along the boardwalk
On a Sunday afternoon.
You may walk the line, walk your talk
Or even walk the moon!

But I walk on the wild side,
And life's crosswalk that I thank
Is that while I dance the "Cake Walk"
I'm not forced to walk the plank!

The Cake Walk

Banana-Fana Cake Roll

MAKES 12 SERVINGS

PREP: 20 MINUTES, PLUS CHILLING

BAKE: AT 375° FOR 10 TO 12 MINUTES

Remember the song "The Name Game"? That's the rhyming game where you make up some of the lyrics, although there are some names you want to stay away from, and you know what they are—I can tell you're smiling. I used the song in my video *Sweatin' to the Oldies III*. Then for the longest time afterwards, I'd wake up every morning with that song stuck in my head. Enough already. How do I turn it off? I know—I'll make a banana cake roll. It'll be like an exorcism. Here's the recipe for that very same cake. But the song's still playing.

Nonstick vegetable-oil cooking spray

CAKE

¾ cup cake flour

½ teaspoon baking soda

¼ teaspoon salt

⅔ cup packed light-brown sugar

1 large whole egg

¾ cup pureed ripe banana (about 2 medium)

1 teaspoon pure vanilla extract

3 large egg whites

FILLING

1 teaspoon unflavored gelatin

¼ cup cold water

1 container (8 ounces) nonfat strawberry yogurt

1 cup frozen reduced-fat nondairy whipped topping, thawed

1½ cups sliced fresh strawberries

1 tablespoon confectioners' sugar, for garnish

1. Preheat oven to 375°. Line 15 × 10-inch jelly-roll pan with aluminum foil, leaving 2-inch overhang all around. Lightly coat with nonstick cooking spray.

2. *Make cake:* Onto sheet of waxed paper, sift together flour, baking soda, and salt.

3. In large bowl, with electric mixer on medium speed, beat together brown sugar and whole egg until light and creamy, about 2 minutes. Beat in banana and vanilla.

4. In clean bowl, with clean beaters, beat egg whites until thick and glossy peaks form. Fold gently into banana mixture. Sprinkle with half the flour mixture and fold in gently. Then add remaining flour mixture and fold in. Pour into prepared pan, smoothing top with rubber spatula and spreading to edges.

5. Bake in 375° oven until top of cake is springy to the touch and lightly browned, 10 to 12 minutes. Remove pan from oven. Loosen foil around edges. Loosely roll up cake, with foil, from a short side so you have a 10-inch-long roll. Transfer foil with cake to wire rack to cool.

6. *Meanwhile, make filling:* In 1-cup glass measure, sprinkle gelatin over ¼ cup cold water. Let stand until softened, 3 minutes. Set glass measure in small saucepan of simmering water and heat, stirring gelatin mixture, until gelatin is dissolved, about 2 minutes. Remove glass measure from water and cool slightly.

7. In medium bowl, stir together yogurt and gelatin mixture. Refrigerate, stirring every 10 minutes, until

mixture begins to thicken and mound, about 20 minutes. Stir until smooth. Fold in whipped topping and then strawberries.

8 Unroll cake with foil. Spread filling over cooled cake, leaving ½-inch border along one short side. Then, lifting up roll from other short side, roll cake up, jelly-roll fashion, discarding foil. Place cake, seam side down, on serving platter. Cover and refrigerate at least 2 hours or up to 8 hours.

9 To serve, dust with confectioners' sugar. Store in refrigerator.

NUTRIENT VALUE PER SERVING OF MY CAKE ROLL

116 calories, 4 g protein, 1 g fat (5% fat; 0 g saturated fat), 25 g carbohydrate, 132 mg sodium, 18 mg cholesterol

TRADITIONAL CAKE ROLL

274 calories (2⅓ times the calories), 15 g fat (15 times the fat)

Centerfold Cheesecakettes

MAKES 12 LITTLE CHEESECAKES

PREP: 20 MINUTES, PLUS CHILLING

BAKE: AT 300° FOR 20 TO 25 MINUTES

*Y*es, all kinds of people come to Slimmons, my exercise studio in Beverly Hills. Even centerfolds, from you-know-which magazine. (Hint: bunny.) And without exception, they always confess to me their biggest downfall is—cheesecake! So, I created this miniature one for centerfolds and wannabe centerfolds everywhere. I wanted to be a centerfold for *Field & Stream*. When they turned me down, I tried *Popular Mechanics*. But anyway, be sure to number these cheesecakes, so you can keep track of how many bunnies—ooops! . . . Centerfold Cheesecakettes you have left.

12 vanilla wafer cookies

1¼ cups low-fat (2%) small-curd cottage cheese

1 package (8 ounces) Neufchâtel cream cheese, at room temperature

¾ cup granulated sugar

3 tablespoons all-purpose flour

3 large egg whites

2 teaspoons grated lemon zest

1 tablespoon fresh lemon juice

1 teaspoon pure vanilla extract

¼ cup blueberry jam

1 Preheat oven to 300°. Line 12 muffin-pan cups (2½ inches) with paper liners. Place one cookie in each cup.

2 In food processor, process cottage cheese until completely smooth, about 2 minutes. Remove cottage cheese to large bowl. In food processor, combine Neufchâtel cream cheese, sugar, and flour, and process until smooth. Stir into pureed cottage cheese. Stir in egg whites, lemon zest, lemon juice, and vanilla, until well blended. Spoon mixture into muffin cups, dividing equally.

3 In small saucepan, gently warm blueberry jam. Spoon 1 teaspoon jam in center of each cheesecake, pushing down slightly into center. Draw table knife through jam to swirl.

4 Bake in 300° oven until cheesecakes are set but still slightly jiggly, 20 to 25 minutes. Let cool completely in pan on wire rack. Cover loosely and refrigerate 4 hours or overnight. Use table knife to gently remove cheesecakes from pan.

NUTRIENT VALUE PER MY CHEESECAKE

163 calories, 7 g protein, 6 g fat (32% fat; 3 g saturated fat), 21g carbohydrate, 202 mg sodium, 16 mg cholesterol

THE TRADITIONAL CHEESECAKE

429 calories (more than 2½ times the calories), 32 g fat (5⅓ times the fat)

It's a Fine-Lime Pound Cake

MAKES 12 SERVINGS

PREP: 20 MINUTES

BAKE: AT 350° FOR 30 TO 35 MINUTES

When you eat a regular pound cake, you're walking a fine line, because you're starting with a pound of butter, a pound of sugar, a pound of . . . , a pound of . . . . But with my cake, you're just eating fine limes, and you'll be divine.

Nonstick vegetable-oil cooking spray

CAKE

1¾ cups cake flour

1 teaspoon baking soda

½ teaspoon salt

1 cup nonfat plain yogurt

¾ cup granulated sugar

2 tablespoons canola oil

2 tablespoons unsalted butter, melted

1 large egg

4 teaspoons grated lime zest

1 tablespoon fresh lime juice

½ teaspoon lemon extract

GLAZE

½ cup <u>sifted</u> confectioners' sugar

2 teaspoons nonfat plain yogurt

1 teaspoon grated lime zest

2 teaspoons fresh lime juice

1. Preheat oven to 350°. Lightly coat 8 × 8 × 2-inch square baking pan with nonstick cooking spray.

2. *Make cake:* In medium bowl, sift together cake flour, baking soda, and salt. In another medium bowl, whisk together yogurt, sugar, oil, butter, egg, lime zest, lime juice, and lemon extract. Stir flour mixture into yogurt mixture until flour is just moistened. Spoon into prepared pan.

3. Bake in 350° oven until golden, and a wooden pick inserted in center comes out clean, 30 to 35 minutes. Cool cake completely in pan on wire rack.

4. *Make glaze:* In small bowl, stir together confectioners' sugar, yogurt, lime zest, and lime juice, until smooth. Spread over top of cooled cake. Let cake stand, uncovered, until glaze is dry to the touch. Then cut into 12 pieces.

NUTRIENT VALUE PER SERVING OF
MY CAKE

179 calories, 3 g protein, 5 g fat (24% fat; 2 g saturated fat), 31 g carbohydrate, 216 mg sodium, 23 mg cholesterol

TRADITIONAL POUND CAKE

316 calories (1¾ times the calories), 12 g fat (almost 2½ times the fat)

yogurt and canola oil

I use just a little Sacred Fat in this recipe—butter. You really can't have a pound cake without it. Then I make up the difference with nonfat yogurt and canola oil.

Two-for-Tea Petits Fours

MAKES 24 TINY, TINY CAKES

PREP: 35 MINUTES, PLUS STANDING

BAKE: AT 350° FOR 18 MINUTES

In New Orleans, there is a famous hotel called the Windsor Court. I loved going there for a quiet tea in the afternoon. Well, I didn't actually go for the tea—I really went for the little petits fours, watercress sandwiches, and the teeny cookies. It's a very dignified, heavily draped room—with a harpist strumming softly in the corner and ladies in hats, brushing crumbs off their white gloves, and no other sound louder than the crunch of a watercress sandwich. Until—I enter, in tank top and shorts, crooning "Tea for two, and two for tea . . . ." My petits fours are the most adorable, bite-size almond layer cakes, with a touch of sweet-tart apricot jam, and topped with an orange glaze.

Nonstick vegetable-oil cooking spray

CAKE

2 tablespoons almond paste

¼ cup granulated sugar

2 large eggs, separated

2 tablespoons canola oil

2 tablespoons low-fat milk (1%)

½ teaspoon pure vanilla extract

7 tablespoons cake flour

Pinch salt

Confectioners' sugar, for dusting

2 tablespoons apricot jam

GLAZE

1½ tablespoons warm water

1½ teaspoons powdered egg whites

1 teaspoon fresh lemon juice

¼ teaspoon orange extract

1½ cups confectioners' sugar

Food colorings, as you like

1 Preheat oven to 350°. Lightly coat 8 × 8 × 2-inch square baking pan with nonstick cooking spray.

2 *Make cake:* Into medium bowl, crumble almond paste. Add granulated sugar and 1 egg yolk and stir until uniform paste forms. Stir in second egg yolk, canola oil, milk, and vanilla. Stir in flour and salt.

3 In another medium bowl, with electric mixer on medium speed, beat egg whites until peaks are stiff and glossy. Fold into flour mixture. Spoon batter into prepared pan and spread evenly.

4 Bake in 350° oven until firm, and a wooden pick inserted in center comes out clean, about 18 minutes. Cool cake in pan on wire rack at least 1 hour, or overnight.

5 Lightly dust top of cake with confectioners' sugar. Invert onto piece of waxed paper. Remove pan. Using long serrated knife, split cake horizontally in half. Place bottom half of cake, cut side up, on cutting board. Spread with apricot jam. Place other half, cut side down, on top.

6 *Make glaze:* In small bowl, stir 1½ tablespoons warm water and powdered whites until dissolved, 2 minutes. Stir in lemon juice and orange extract. Stir in confectioners' sugar. Set aside 2 tablespoons glaze and tint with a drop of food coloring. Tint remainder with different color. (Use several colors, if you like, but keep it subtle.) With metal spatula, spread larger amount of glaze over top of cake.

7 With small sharp knife, score top of cake into 24 small rectangles. Spoon remaining glaze into pastry bag fitted with small writing tip, or into small plastic food-storage bag, with ⅛ inch of corner snipped off. Decorate top of cake as 24 individual cakes between scored marks. Leave cake out, uncovered, at room temperature to let glaze dry at least 6 hours, or overnight.

8 Using long serrated knife, first trim edges. Then cut cake along scored marks into 24 rectangles. Wipe knife clean between each cut. Arrange on plates.

NUTRIENT VALUE PER MY PETIT FOUR

68 calories, 1 g protein, 2 g fat (26% fat; 0 g saturated fat), 12 g carbohydrate, 14 mg sodium, 18 mg cholesterol

TRADITIONAL PETIT FOUR

198 calories (almost 3 times the calories), 3 g fat (1½ times the fat)

You Bet Your Sweet Bundt

MAKES 16 SERVINGS

PREP: 20 MINUTES

BAKE: AT 350° FOR 55 MINUTES

A bundt cake is everyone's favorite—it's round, it's high, and it has curvy sides where icing can cascade down like a waterfall. I marbleize mine. People always ask me how I do that. Do you cut out these separate pieces and then stick them all together to make this cake? Are there little pieces of Scotch tape hidden everywhere? If I look underneath, will I find Popsicle sticks holding the whole thing together? Well, read on and you'll learn how to marbleize.

Nonstick vegetable-oil cooking spray

2¼ cups cake flour

2 teaspoons baking powder

½ teaspoon baking soda

¼ teaspoon salt

6 tablespoons (¾ stick) 70% buttermilk-vegetable oil spread, at room temperature

1½ cups granulated sugar

1 large whole egg

2 large egg whites

1 teaspoon pure vanilla extract

⅓ cup unsweetened cocoa powder

2 tablespoons light-brown sugar

½ teaspoon ground cinnamon

⅓ cup water

1 cup low-fat buttermilk

1. Preheat oven to 350°. Lightly coat 10-inch bundt pan with nonstick cooking spray.

2. Into large bowl, sift together cake flour, baking powder, baking soda, and salt.

3. In medium bowl, with electric mixer on medium speed, beat vegetable oil spread until smooth and creamy. Add granulated sugar and beat until well combined. Add whole egg and beat until light and fluffy. Beat in egg whites, one at a time, until very light (mixture may appear curdled, but don't be concerned; that's the way it should look). Beat in vanilla.

4. In small bowl, stir together cocoa powder, brown sugar, cinnamon, and ⅓ cup water, until smooth. Set aside.

5. Into egg mixture, alternately fold flour mixture and buttermilk, beginning and ending with flour mixture. Spoon two-thirds of mixture into prepared pan. Stir cocoa mixture into remaining egg mixture until well combined. Spoon cocoa batter in dollops over batter in pan. With small metal spatula or table knife, make swirls in batter, combining vanilla and chocolate batters to create marbled effect.

6. Bake in 350° oven until a wooden pick inserted near center comes out clean, about 55 minutes. Cool cake in pan on wire rack. Loosen sides with spatula and invert onto serving plate. Remove pan.

NUTRIENT VALUE PER SERVING OF
MY BUNDT CAKE

184 calories, 3 g protein, 5 g fat (22% fat; 1 g saturated fat), 34 g carbohydrate, 184 mg sodium, 14 mg cholesterol

THE CLASSIC BUNDT CAKE
219 calories (1⅕ times the calories),
7 g fat (almost 1½ times the fat)

Walnut-Sour Cream Gems

MAKES 24 MINI CUPCAKES

PREP: 30 MINUTES

BAKE: AT 350° FOR 18 MINUTES

Shhh!—there's a secret ingredient in these gems. No, no—don't even look at the recipe. Just keep reading this. If I told you what the ingredient was, you wouldn't believe it. So here's what I want you to do. Go to a friend or loved one. Have them read the recipe and then make the gems for you. Now pop one in your mouth. What is that rich, moist taste? Now you can read the recipe.

GEMS

½ cup (2 ounces) snipped prunes
3 tablespoons hot water
Nonstick vegetable-oil cooking spray
1 cup cake flour
1½ teaspoons ground cinnamon
1 teaspoon baking powder
½ teaspoon baking soda
¼ teaspoon salt
1 large egg
1 tablespoon canola oil
½ cup packed light-brown sugar
1 teaspoon pure vanilla extract
½ cup reduced-fat sour cream
¼ cup + 4 teaspoons finely chopped walnuts
1 tablespoon granulated sugar

MOLASSES FROSTING

¾ cup confectioners' sugar
1 tablespoon unsalted butter, at room temperature
1½ teaspoons molasses
½ teaspoon pure vanilla extract
Pinch salt
2 teaspoons low-fat milk (1%), plus up to 1 teaspoon more as needed

1 Make gems: In small bowl, soak prunes in 3 tablespoons hot water to soften, about 20 minutes.

2 Preheat oven to 350°. Lightly coat 24 mini-muffin-pan cups (2 pans) with nonstick cooking spray (or bake two batches using one pan).

3 In small bowl, stir together flour, 1 teaspoon cinnamon, the baking powder, baking soda, and salt.

4 In medium bowl, whisk together egg, oil, brown sugar, and vanilla, until blended. Alternately stir flour mixture and sour cream into egg mixture, until flour mixture is just moistened. Stir in prunes with

any soaking liquid and ¼ cup walnuts. Spoon batter into prepared muffin-pan cups.

5 In small bowl, stir together remaining 4 teaspoons walnuts, the granulated sugar, and remaining ½ teaspoon cinnamon. Sprinkle over batter in cups.

6 Bake in 350° oven until golden brown and slightly puffed, about 18 minutes. Let gems cool in pans on rack for 5 minutes. Remove gems to rack to cool.

7 Make frosting: In small bowl, combine confectioners' sugar, butter, molasses, vanilla, salt, and 2 teaspoons milk. With electric mixer on low speed, beat until combined. Then increase mixer speed to medium and beat until smooth. Add remaining milk, if needed, until it reaches good spreading consistency. You should have about ½ cup frosting.

8 When gems are cool, spread 1 teaspoon frosting over each. Or spoon frosting into pastry bag fitted with small writing tip, or into small plastic food-storage bag with ⅛ inch of corner snipped off, and pipe designs over tops.

NUTRIENT VALUE PER MY GEM, WITHOUT FROSTING

82 calories, 2 g protein, 3 g fat (32% fat; 1 g saturated fat), 12 g carbohydrate, 96 mg sodium, 14 mg cholesterol

WITH FROSTING

106 calories, 2 g protein, 4 g fat (30% fat; 1 g saturated fat), 17 g carbohydrate, 103 mg sodium, 16 mg cholesterol

TRADITIONAL CUPCAKE WITH FROSTING

460 calories (4⅓ times the calories), 17 g fat (4¼ times the fat)

IS THIS A CUPCAKE OR A MUFFIN?

Neither—it's a gem. Why? The tiny pans I use for baking these delectable little jewels are called gem pans. So I call them gems. Others with less romance in their soul would call them mini cupcakes.

Have You Athena Baklava?

PREP: 30 MINUTES

BAKE: AT 325° FOR 50 TO 55 MINUTES

COOK: 4 MINUTES

Everywhere you go in Athens, someone is selling baklava. Next to the souvenir stands, there's baklava. In the churches, there's baklava. On the buses, there's baklava. Well, after eating twenty-three pieces, I just fainted dead away in the Acropolis, in front of the statue of Athena. When I came to, I had a vision—baklava with grapenuts. And as I stared at Athena's feet, I knew what I was going to call my baklava.

PASTRY

3 tablespoons 70% buttermilk-vegetable oil spread

½ cup walnut pieces

½ cup blanched almonds

⅓ cup granulated sugar

⅔ cup grapenuts cereal

2 tablespoons sesame seeds, *lightly toasted*

1 teaspoon ground cinnamon

Nonstick butter-flavored cooking spray

Twenty-two sheets (13 × 9 inches) frozen phyllo dough, *thawed according to package directions*

SYRUP

⅔ cup granulated sugar

⅔ cup water

3 strips (3 × ½-inch each) orange zest

2 tablespoons fresh lemon juice

⅛ teaspoon ground cloves

1 Place oven rack in lowest position. Preheat oven to 325°.

2 *Make pastry:* In small saucepan or skillet, melt vegetable oil spread over low heat. Set aside.

3 In food processor, combine walnuts, almonds, and sugar and pulse with on/off motion until coarsely ground. Add grapenuts, sesame seeds, and cinnamon. Pulse until finely ground.

4 Coat 9 × 9 × 2-inch square metal baking pan with nonstick cooking spray. Place phyllo on clean, dry surface. Cover lightly with waxed paper and then with a slightly dampened towel, to prevent drying out. Working quickly, stack 3 phyllo sheets in prepared pan, lightly coating top of each sheet with nonstick cooking spray, and leaving slight overhang. Repeat process of coating and stacking next 3 sheets of phyllo, laying them at a right angle across first stack. Lift overhang in and fold down against sides of pan. Sprinkle one-third of nut mixture over phyllo. Drizzle with 2 teaspoons melted vegetable oil spread.

5 Repeat coating and stacking with 5 more sheets. Sprinkle with half the remaining nut mixture, and drizzle with 2 teaspoons melted vegetable oil spread. Lightly coat and stack 5 more phyllo sheets. Top with remaining nuts, and drizzle with 2 more teaspoons melted vegetable oil spread. Lightly coat and stack remaining 6 phyllo sheets on top. Using sharp knife, cut into 16 squares. Cut each square diagonally into 2 triangles. Brush with remaining melted vegetable oil spread.

My baklava is filled with a mixture of walnuts, almonds, and sesame seeds. Grapenuts give the crunch of nuts without the fat. While many baklava are drenched in a honey syrup, mine is soaked in an orange-scented sugar syrup.

NUTRIENT VALUE PER PIECE OF MY BAKLAVA

107 calories, 2 g protein, 4 g fat (34% fat; 1g saturated fat), 16 g carbohydrate, 88 mg sodium, 0 mg cholesterol

TRADITIONAL BAKLAVA

147 calories (1⅓ times the calories), 10 g fat (2½ times the fat)

6 Bake on lowest oven rack in 325° oven until top of phyllo is crisp and golden, 50 to 55 minutes.

7 *Meanwhile, make syrup:* In medium saucepan, stir together sugar, ⅔ cup water, orange zest, lemon juice, and cloves. Bring to a boil. Reduce heat to simmer and cook until slightly reduced, about 4 minutes. Cool. When cool, remove and discard orange zest. Pour cooled syrup over warm pastry. Let stand until completely cold.

"*I'm Late, I'm Late*" Carrot Cake

MAKES 9 SERVINGS

PREP: **20** MINUTES

BAKE: AT **350°** FOR **40** TO **45** MINUTES

I was one of the late ones to jump on the carrot cake bandwagon. When I first heard of zucchini cake and carrot cake and chocolate-beet cake, I thought, Please—why do we have to put vegetables in a dessert? Let's just leave them on the plate where they're perfectly happy by themselves. But then one afternoon I was walking by a bakery shop on Melrose, and in the window I saw a carrot cake with a creamy white frosting, decorated with little frosting carrots. Okay. Let's see what it's all about, Bugsy. I took a bite, cream cheese frosting and all, and my eyes rolled back in my head and my ears grew long and fuzzy. All I could taste was the delicious natural sweetness from the carrots. I just couldn't believe it! I was converted. In my re-creation here, I don't even add granulated sugar, just a little honey. And—surprise!—I use whole-wheat flour.

Nonstick vegetable-oil cooking spray
3 cups grated carrots (about 9 carrots)
¾ cup all-purpose flour
½ cup whole-wheat flour
1 teaspoon baking soda
1 teaspoon ground cinnamon
½ teaspoon salt
¼ teaspoon ground ginger
Pinch ground cloves
¾ cup honey
¼ cup canola oil
1 large whole egg
2 large egg whites
1 tablespoon fresh lemon juice
⅓ cup dried currants or raisins
Frosting (optional, recipe follows)

1 Preheat oven to 350°. Lightly coat bottom of 8 × 8 × 2-inch square cake pan or 9-inch round layer-cake pan with nonstick cooking spray. Line bottom of pan with waxed paper. Lightly coat paper and sides of pan with nonstick cooking spray.

2 Spread grated carrots between sheets of paper towels and squeeze out excess liquid.

3 In small bowl, stir together both flours, baking soda, cinnamon, salt, ginger, and cloves.

4 In large bowl, with electric mixer on medium speed, beat honey, oil, whole egg, egg whites, and lemon juice, until well blended. By hand, stir in flour mix-

ture, carrots, and currants. Scrape batter into prepared pan, and spread evenly with rubber spatula.

5 Bake in 350° oven until a wooden pick inserted in center of cake comes out clean, 40 to 45 minutes. Cool cake in pan on wire rack for 10 minutes. Turn cake out of pan and cool completely on wire rack. Discard waxed paper.

6 Meanwhile, make frosting, if using, and spread over top of cake. Cut into 9 squares or wedges and serve.

FROSTING

In medium bowl, with electric mixer on medium speed, beat together 4 ounces room-temperature Neufchâtel cream cheese, 2½ tablespoons honey, and 1½ teaspoons pure vanilla extract, until smooth and blended. Cover, and chill until it reaches good spreading consistency.

NUTRIENT VALUE PER SERVING OF
MY CAKE, WITHOUT FROSTING
244 calories, 4 g protein, 6 g fat (22% fat; 1 g saturated fat), 44 g carbohydrate, 293 mg sodium, 24 mg cholesterol

WITH FROSTING
296 calories, 5 g protein, 10 g fat (30% fat; 3 g saturated fat), 50 g carbohydrate, 343 mg sodium, 33 mg cholesterol

TRADITIONAL CARROT CAKE WITH FROSTING
650 calories (more than twice the calories), 33 g fat (3⅓ times the fat)

CARROT TOP

Make an additional one-half recipe of frosting. Tint two-thirds orange for carrot decoration, and one-third green for carrot tops. Then spread white frosting over top of cake. Using a pastry bag fitted with a small writing tip, or plastic food-storage bag with ⅛ inch of corner snipped off, pipe on carrots. Then finish with green carrot tops.

What-Goes-Up-Must-Come-Down Chocolate Torte Cakes

MAKES 6 INDIVIDUAL TORTES

PREP: 20 MINUTES

BAKE: AT 375° FOR 13 TO 16 MINUTES

These are actually individual soufflés that puff right up. But wait a second—oh, no! They collapse right away. Don't feel guilty, or cry, "What did I do wrong, Argentina?" That's what they're supposed to do. When you get an F on your cooking report card for this, it's really an A. The F is for "fallen," which makes the cake rich and fudgy in the center, tasting like it has a zillion more calories than it does.

CAKES

¼ cup packed light-brown sugar

¼ cup unsweetened cocoa powder

2 tablespoons boiling water

1 ounce semisweet chocolate, chopped

½ teaspoon pure vanilla extract

2 large eggs, separated

2 tablespoons all-purpose flour

Pinch salt

2 tablespoons granulated sugar

SAUCE

1 can (15¼ ounces) pear halves, in juice

Reduced-fat sour cream, for garnish (optional)

1. Preheat oven to 375°. Line 6 Texas-size (3½ × 1¾ inches) or jumbo muffin-pan cups with paper liners.

2. Make cakes: In small saucepan, stir together brown sugar, cocoa powder, and 2 tablespoons boiling water, until smooth. Add chopped chocolate and stir over low heat until just melted. Add vanilla. Remove from heat.

3. In medium bowl, with electric mixer on medium speed, beat egg yolks until lemon-colored. Drizzle in melted chocolate mixture, whisking to prevent eggs from curdling. Whisk in flour until just blended.

4. In clean medium bowl, with clean beaters on medium speed, beat egg whites just until frothy. Continue beating until soft peaks form. Add salt and then gradually beat in granulated sugar. Continue beating until stiff and glossy peaks form. Stir one-quarter of beaten egg whites into chocolate mixture to lighten. Fold in remaining whites until just blended and no white streaks remain. Divide batter equally among the 6 prepared muffin-pan cups.

5. Bake in 375° oven until puffy, and a wooden pick inserted in centers comes out clean, 13 to 16 minutes. Cool tortes in muffin-pan cups briefly on wire rack.

6. Meanwhile, make sauce: Drain pear halves, reserving ⅓ cup juice. In blender or food processor, puree pears until smooth, adding reserved juice.

7. Carefully remove warm individual chocolate tortes from muffin-pan cups and peel off paper liners. Spoon some pear sauce on each of 6 dessert plates. Place each warm torte on a plate in sauce. Spoon a little sour cream on top, if you'd like.

the secret's in the chocolate

Just look at all the fat and calorie savings in this one! I use whole eggs, but fewer than in a regular soufflé, and cocoa powder has fewer calories and much less fat than regular chocolate, which is full of cocoa butter. But I still managed to sneak in a small amount of chocolate.

NUTRIENT VALUE PER MY TORTE
159 calories, 4 g protein, 4 g fat (22% fat; 2 g saturated fat), 31 g carbohydrate, 49 mg sodium, 71 mg cholesterol

THE USUAL SOUFFLÉ
795 calories (5 times the calories), 40 g fat (10 times the fat)

Pear-Cranberry Upside-Down Cake

MAKES 10 SERVINGS

PREP: 20 MINUTES

BAKE: AT 350° FOR 35 TO 40 MINUTES

Fill in the blank: Pineapple _____ Cake. You got it! Upside-down! See, you could be a contestant on "Wheel of Fortune." Watch out, Vanna! Originally, this was a right-side-up cake and made with different fruit. In the early 1800s, a frontier housewife made a special cake with pears and cranberries for her husband, to celebrate a successful hunting trip. As she carried it to the table in the dim firelight, she tripped on a loose floorboard. The cake flew across the room, landing perfectly in the center of the empty platter on the table, upside down. Her husband exclaimed, "Wow, what a pretty cake!" And that's how a tripped-up cake became a culinary icon.

3 tablespoons light butter, at room temperature

⅓ cup packed light-brown sugar

2 firm-ripe Bartlett pears, peeled, quartered, and cored, and each quarter cut lengthwise into 3 wedges

1 cup fresh or frozen cranberries, not thawed

1 cup all-purpose flour

1½ teaspoons baking powder

¼ teaspoon salt

1 large egg white

1 large whole egg, separated

½ cup granulated sugar

2 teaspoons pure vanilla extract

⅓ cup low-fat milk (1%)

1 teaspoon grated orange zest

1 Preheat oven to 350°.

2 In 10-inch cast-iron skillet or other heavy 10-inch ovenproof skillet, melt 1 tablespoon light butter over medium heat. Brush melted butter to coat bottom and halfway up sides of skillet. Remove from heat. Sprinkle bottom evenly with brown sugar. In bottom of skillet, arrange pear wedges, rounded side down, like spokes of a wheel, leaving center open. Fill in center and spaces between pears with cranberries.

3 In small bowl, stir together flour, baking powder, and salt.

4 In medium bowl, with electric mixer on medium speed, beat egg whites until foamy. Gradually beat in ¼ cup granulated sugar. Increase mixer speed to medium-high and beat until stiff and glossy peaks form.

5 In large bowl, combine remaining 2 tablespoons light butter, remaining ¼ cup granulated sugar, the egg yolk, and vanilla. With electric mixer on medium speed, beat until blended, about 2 minutes. Beat in

half the milk. Reduce mixer speed to low and beat in half the flour mixture. Beat in remaining milk, the orange zest, and then remaining flour mixture. Stir in spoonful of beaten egg whites to lighten mixture. Gently fold in remaining whites in two additions, just until blended. Pour batter evenly over pears in skillet.

6 Bake in 350° oven until a wooden pick inserted in center comes out clean, 35 to 40 minutes. Transfer skillet to wire rack to cool for 3 minutes. Invert serving plate over skillet. Using mitts to protect your hands, carefully invert cake onto plate. Remove skillet. Spread any glaze remaining in skillet over pears. Let cake cool completely.

NUTRIENT VALUE PER SERVING OF MY UPSIDE-DOWN CAKE

170 calories, 3 g protein, 4 g fat (21% fat; 1 g saturated fat), 31 g carbohydrate, 162 mg sodium, 22 mg cholesterol

FRONTIER-WOMAN UPSIDE-DOWN CAKE

325 calories (almost twice the calories), 10 g fat (more than twice the fat)

oh, what a pear!

BARTLETT, with a red or yellow skin, and a hint of green, is perfect for all kinds of cooking—it wins the medal for best all-around pear. **ANJOU,** another good all-purpose pear but harder to find, is round with a short neck, with a thin yellow-green skin. **BOSC** is very crisp, light brownish-orange, and long-necked. It's a poacher, and also good for sautéing. Another good poacher is **COMICE,** short and very round, with light greenish-brown skin.

Tangerine-Dream Poppy-Seed Cake

MAKES 16 SERVINGS

PREP: 20 MINUTES

BAKE: AT 350° FOR 40 TO 45 MINUTES

Take a nibble of this cake, close your eyes, and you'll dream you're in old Tangier, surrounded by baskets of fragrant tangerines. Move your dream just a little to the left—see those fields of poppies? That's where poppy seeds come from. And these seeds are tiny. How tiny? Would you believe 900,000 in a pound. That's about 100,000, give or take, in one of those little spice jars. So be careful—don't knock the jar over! (I've done that already.) And after eating a piece of this cake, whatever you do, don't smile until you floss, or people will smile at you.

Nonstick vegetable-oil cooking spray

CAKE

2¼ cups cake flour

1½ teaspoons baking powder

½ teaspoon baking soda

Pinch salt

⅓ cup 70% buttermilk-vegetable oil spread, at room temperature

1⅓ cups granulated sugar

2 large whole eggs

1 large egg white

4 teaspoons grated tangerine or orange zest

2 teaspoons poppy seeds

1 cup low-fat buttermilk

2 tablespoons frozen tangerine or orange juice concentrate, thawed

GLAZE

1 teaspoon water

¾ teaspoon frozen tangerine or orange juice concentrate, thawed

½ teaspoon grated tangerine or orange zest

About ¼ cup confectioners' sugar

1. Preheat oven to 350°. Lightly coat 10-inch bundt pan with nonstick cooking spray.

2. *Make cake:* Into medium bowl, sift together flour, baking powder, baking soda, and salt.

3. In large bowl, with electric mixer on medium speed, beat vegetable oil spread until smooth and creamy, 1 to 2 minutes. Beat in granulated sugar until well blended. Beat in whole eggs, one at a time. Beat in egg white. Beat in zest and poppy seeds.

4. In small bowl, stir together buttermilk and tangerine juice concentrate. Alternately fold flour mixture and buttermilk mixture into egg mixture, beginning and ending with flour mixture, until just blended. Do not overmix. Pour batter into prepared bundt pan and rap pan gently on counter to remove any air pockets.

5. Bake in 350° oven until cake begins to pull away from side of pan, and a wooden pick inserted near center comes out clean, 40 to 45 minutes. Transfer pan to wire rack to cool for about 10 minutes. With small knife, gently loosen sides of cake and invert onto rack. Remove pan. Let cool completely.

6. *Make glaze:* In small bowl, stir 1 teaspoon water, tangerine juice concentrate, and zest. Stir in confectioners' sugar until just pourable. Drizzle over cake.

TANGERINE— WHAT'S IN A NAME?

The tangerine is really a
mandarin orange, but it's named
after Tangier, in Morocco.
(If you were from Tangier, you'd
be a Tangerine, too.) It has a
sweet taste, and it's loose-skinned
for easy peeling—so don't worry,
you won't break a nail.

Upside-Down Baby Cakes

MAKES 6 INDIVIDUAL CAKES

PREP: 20 MINUTES

BAKE: AT 350° FOR 25 MINUTES

You know what happens to Baby Cabbage-Patch Dolls—they grow up to be big dolls. Well, the same thing happens with cakes. My little baby pineapple cakes grow up to be big ones, but I love them when they're small. You know why? I can eat the whole thing, and it's still just one serving. I love having my very own cake (and eating it, too). There are some things I just don't want to share.

Nonstick vegetable-oil cooking spray

12 pineapple slices, in juice (from two 20-ounce cans)

¼ cup packed light-brown sugar

6 macadamia nuts

¾ cup cake flour

1 teaspoon baking powder

¼ teaspoon salt

2 tablespoons light butter, at room temperature

½ cup granulated sugar

1 large egg

1 teaspoon pure vanilla extract

¼ cup low-fat milk (1%)

1 Preheat oven to 350°. Lightly coat 6 Texas-size (3½ × 1¾ inches) or jumbo muffin-pan cups with nonstick cooking spray.

2 Pat pineapple slices dry with paper towels. Place 2 pineapple slices in bottom of each prepared muffin-pan cup. Sprinkle pineapple with brown sugar. Place one macadamia nut in center of each.

3 In small bowl, stir together cake flour, baking powder, and salt. In medium bowl, with electric mixer on medium speed, beat butter, granulated sugar, egg, and vanilla, until well blended, about 2 minutes. Reduce mixer speed to low and alternately beat flour mixture and milk into butter mixture in three additions, beginning and ending with flour mixture, until just blended. Spoon batter into prepared cups, dividing equally.

4 Bake in 350° oven until a wooden pick inserted in centers comes out clean, about 25 minutes. Run knife around sides of cakes. While cakes are still hot, using oven mitts, place baking sheet over muffin pan and invert onto baking sheet. Remove pan. Spoon any glaze remaining in muffin-pan cups over cakes. Let cool completely before serving.

NUTRIENT VALUE PER MY BABY CAKE

274 calories, 3 g protein, 6 g fat (20% fat; 1 g saturated fat), 55 g carbohydrate, 209 mg sodium, 36 mg cholesterol

TRADITIONAL PINEAPPLE

UPSIDE-DOWN CAKE

325 calories (1⅕ times calories), 10 g fat (1⅔ times the fat)

hawaii's nut

Macadamia nuts taste so buttery, and slightly sweet—so who needs butter? But watch out—22 grams of fat per ounce. Here's another one of those nuts you want to keep locked up in the refrigerator so it doesn't go rancid.

Easy-Iced Chocolate Layer Cake

MAKES 16 SERVINGS

PREP: 30 MINUTES

BAKE: AT 375° FOR 35 MINUTES

Tell the truth—I bet you've had some icing disasters you've never shared with anyone. Well I've had a whole bunch. Once, for my housekeeper Teresa's birthday, I used so much icing for the cake, the top layer slid right off, just like a house in Malibu. For another birthday, I made the icing too thin—it looked like the poor thing had been left out in the rain. But you know what my usual problem is? I run out of icing. I eat as I spread—one spread for the cake, one for me, one for the cake. You get the picture—after I finish frosting the top, there's none left for the sides. But then I decided maybe this is not such a bad thing. Less icing means fewer calories and fat. So for this cake, I've made enough to spread between the layers and do the top, and that's it.

Nonstick vegetable-oil cooking spray

CAKE

2 cups cake flour
¾ cup unsweetened cocoa powder
1 tablespoon baking powder
Pinch salt
¼ cup (½ stick) 70% buttermilk-vegetable oil spread, at room temperature
1¾ cups granulated sugar
3 large egg whites
1½ teaspoons pure vanilla extract
2 cups low-fat buttermilk

ORANGE ICING

1½ cups confectioners' sugar
¼ cup orange marmalade
2 tablespoons 70% buttermilk-vegetable oil spread
1 tablespoon low-fat milk (1%)
½ teaspoon fresh lemon juice
¼ teaspoon orange extract

1 Preheat oven to 375°. Lightly coat two 8-inch round layer-cake pans with nonstick cooking spray.

2 *Make cake:* In small bowl, stir together flour, cocoa powder, baking powder, and salt.

3 In medium bowl, with electric mixer on medium speed, beat together vegetable oil spread and sugar, until well blended. Stir in egg whites and vanilla. Alternately stir in flour mixture and buttermilk until smooth, beginning and ending with flour mixture. Divide equally between prepared pans.

4 Bake in 375° oven until firm, and a wooden pick inserted in centers comes out covered with crumbs, about 35 minutes. Cool cakes completely in pans on wire rack.

5 *Make icing:* In medium bowl, combine confectioners' sugar, marmalade, vegetable oil spread, milk, lemon juice, and orange extract. With electric mixer on medium speed, beat until smooth.

6 Unmold cakes. Place one layer, top side up, on serving platter. Spread with half the icing. Cover with second layer, top side up. Spread with remaining icing.

NUTRIENT VALUE PER SERVING OF

MY CHOCOLATE LAYER CAKE

243 calories, 4 g protein, 5 g fat (19% fat; 1 g saturated fat),

49 g carbohydrate, 162 mg sodium, 1 mg cholesterol

TRADITIONAL CHOCOLATE LAYER CAKE

694 calories (almost 3 times the calories),

42 g fat (more than 8 times the fat)

final flourish

This is where a strip zester comes in handy. No, it's not a nightclub act. It's a little hand tool with a notched hole on the end. When you run this across the surface of an orange, you get a gorgeous orange curlicue you can use as a pretty garnish.

Rainbow Cake

MAKES 14 SERVINGS

PREP: 1 HOUR

BAKE: AT 350° FOR 30 MINUTES

I spend a lot of time at 35,000 feet, staring out a little window. When I first started thinking about this book, instead of clouds I would see visions of low-fat éclairs, chocolate mousse pie, and cannolis.

And then there it was—the most beautiful rainbow. The angels were baking. That's it! It hit me like a thunderbolt. I'll make a rainbow cake with all its fabulous colors, and bring it to earth. Oh thank you, angels, for the inspiration. And you can be sure, there's no pot of fat at the end of this one.

Nonstick vegetable-oil cooking spray

CAKE

1½ cups cake flour

1 teaspoon baking powder

½ teaspoon baking soda

¼ teaspoon salt

¼ cup (½ stick) 70% buttermilk-vegetable oil spread,
   at room temperature

1 cup granulated sugar

1 large egg, separated

1 teaspoon pure vanilla extract

1 large egg white

⅔ cup low-fat buttermilk

½ cup flaked sweetened coconut

FROSTING

3 cups confectioners' sugar

¼ cup (½ stick) 70% buttermilk-vegetable oil spread

2 teaspoons pure vanilla extract

½ teaspoon rum extract

¼ teaspoon salt

2 tablespoons low-fat milk (1%)

Red, yellow, green, and blue food colorings

1 Preheat oven to 350°. Lightly coat 9-inch spring-form pan with nonstick cooking spray.

2 Make cake: In medium bowl, stir together flour, baking powder, baking soda, and salt.

3 In large bowl, with mixer on medium speed, beat vegetable oil spread until smooth. Beat in sugar until blended. Beat in egg yolk until light, then vanilla.

4 In a separate bowl, with clean beaters, beat egg whites on medium-high until soft peaks form.

5 Alternately fold flour mixture and buttermilk into yolk mixture, beginning and ending with flour. Fold in egg whites and coconut. Pour into prepared pan.

6 Bake in 350° oven until firm, and a wooden pick inserted in center comes out clean, about 30 minutes. Cool cake in pan on wire rack.

7 Make frosting: In bowl, mix sugar, vegetable oil spread, vanilla and rum extracts, and salt. Add 1 tablespoon milk. With mixer on medium speed, beat until smooth and fluffy. Stir in enough milk to make mixture spreadable, about 1 tablespoon more.

8 Place 2 tablespoons frosting in small bowl and tint pink with 1 drop red food coloring. In another bowl, tint 3 tablespoons frosting yellow. Then tint ¼ cup frosting green and the remaining frosting light blue.

9 Assemble cake: Remove cake from pan. Cut cake vertically in half through center to make two half-moons. Using 3-inch-diameter round cutter, cut out half moon from straight side of each cake half to make rainbow shape. (You will not need the cutouts for this recipe, but you can glue the two semicircles together with a little frosting, and then cover the outside with yellow frosting. Say hello to Mr. Sun!) Spread 2 tablespoons blue frosting across the flat top of one cake half. Stack other cake half on top and press to "glue" together. Place on serving platter. Spread all vertical sides (including cutout side) with blue frosting. Spread pink frosting into 1-inch-wide strip to form shortest arc of rainbow. Follow with yellow arc, then green.

**NUTRIENT VALUE PER SERVING OF
MY RAINBOW CAKE**

254 calories, 2 g protein, 7 g fat (25% fat; 2 g saturated fat), 46 g carbohydrate, 232 mg sodium, 16 mg cholesterol

**THE USUAL COCONUT CAKE (I'VE NEVER SEEN
A RAINBOW CAKE BEFORE) WITH FROSTING**

575 calories (more than twice the calories), 26 g fat (almost 4 times the fat)

Coney Island Cone Cakes

MAKES 6 INDIVIDUAL CAKE CONES

PREP: 20 MINUTES

BAKE: AT 375° FOR 35 MINUTES

You know what I like about these ice cream cones? They don't melt. I can eat one while riding the roller coaster at Coney Island without getting goop all over my tank top—the ice cream is really chocolate cake, disguised as an ice cream cone. Use sprinkles to decorate the tops, spelling out your name, making a smiley face, or re-creating your favorite historical scenes such as the Last Supper or the Signing of the Declaration of Independence.

CAKE

⅔ cup cake flour

⅓ cup unsweetened cocoa powder

1 teaspoon baking powder

Pinch salt

2 tablespoons 70% buttermilk-vegetable oil spread, at room temperature

½ cup granulated sugar

1 large egg white

½ teaspoon pure vanilla extract

⅔ cup low-fat buttermilk

6 flat-bottomed wafer ice cream cones (3 inches high, 2¼ inches across top)

FROSTING

¾ cup confectioners' sugar

1 tablespoon 70% buttermilk-vegetable oil spread, at room temperature

1 teaspoon low-fat buttermilk

¾ teaspoon pure vanilla extract

Sprinkles in assorted colors and shapes

1 Preheat oven to 375°.

2 *Make cake:* In small bowl, stir together flour, cocoa powder, baking powder, and salt.

3 In medium bowl, with electric mixer on medium speed, beat together vegetable oil spread and sugar, until well blended. Stir in egg white and vanilla. Alternately stir in flour mixture and buttermilk, beginning and ending with flour mixture, until smooth. Spoon into wafer cones to within ½ inch of top. Set on baking sheet.

4 Bake in 375° oven until tops are firm, and a wooden pick inserted in centers comes out covered with crumbs, about 35 minutes. Cool on wire rack.

5 *Make frosting:* In small bowl, combine confectioners' sugar, vegetable oil spread, buttermilk, and vanilla. With electric mixer on medium speed, beat until smooth. Frost tops of cakes. Decorate with sprinkles, to make faces, stripes, patterns, or whatever else you'd like.

NUTRIENT VALUE PER MY CONE CAKE

246 calories, 4 g protein, 6 g fat (22% fat; 2 g saturated fat), 46 g carbohydrate, 178 mg sodium, 1 mg cholesterol

THE USUAL ICE CREAM CONE

442 calories (1¾ times the calories), 26 g fat (4⅓ times the fat)

HOW DO I DO IT?

Instead of regular chocolate, I use unsweetened cocoa powder, from which most of the fatty cocoa butter has been eliminated. And there are no whole eggs in this cake—just 1 egg white, and low-fat buttermilk for richness.

Little Crown Cakes

MAKES 6 MINI BUNDT CAKES

PREP: 30 MINUTES

BAKE: AT 350° FOR 14 TO 16 MINUTES

There once was a king named Randy, and he had the most magnificent crown. A royal prince, Sandy, was born, and when he was three he asked, "Daddy, why can't I have a crown? You walk around with one, and I have nothing to wear!" So the King ordered a crown for the Prince's birthday, and summoned the royal baker to create a mini crown cake for each place setting at the royal birthday table. Now with my recipe, you, too, can have your very own crown.

Nonstick vegetable-oil cooking spray

CAKES

1 cup cake flour

⅔ cup + 1 tablespoon granulated sugar

1 teaspoon baking powder

½ teaspoon baking soda

¼ teaspoon salt

½ cup low-fat buttermilk

¼ cup fat-free liquid egg substitute, thawed if frozen

1½ teaspoons pure vanilla extract

2 large egg whites

⅛ teaspoon cream of tartar

GLAZE

3 to 4 tablespoons low-fat milk (1%)

1 cup confectioners' sugar

1 Preheat oven to 350°. Lightly coat 6 mini-bundt-cake molds with nonstick cooking spray.

2 *Make cakes:* In large bowl, whisk together cake flour, ⅔ cup sugar, baking powder, baking soda, and salt. Whisk in buttermilk, egg substitute, and vanilla, until smooth.

3 In small bowl, with electric mixer on medium-high speed, beat together egg whites and cream of tartar until soft peaks form. Increase mixer speed to high, and beat in remaining 1 tablespoon sugar until stiff and glossy peaks form. Stir large spoonful of whites into batter to lighten. Fold in remaining whites.

4 Scrape batter into prepared pans.

5 Bake in 350° oven until a wooden pick inserted in centers comes out clean, 14 to 16 minutes. Cool cakes in pans on wire racks for 5 minutes. Loosen edges of cakes with small table knife. Invert cakes onto racks, remove pans, and cool completely.

6 *Make glaze:* In small bowl, gradually whisk enough milk into confectioners' sugar until it reaches good glazing consistency.

7 Drizzle glaze over bundt cakes and serve.

NUTRIENT VALUE PER MY MINI BUNDT CAKE, WITHOUT GLAZE

185 calories, 5 g protein, 1 g fat (5% fat; 0 g saturated fat), 40 g carbohydrate, 316 mg sodium, 1 mg cholesterol

WITH GLAZE

266 calories, 5 g protein, 2 g fat (5% fat; 0 g saturated fat), 59 g carbohydrate, 340 mg sodium, 1 mg cholesterol

AN ORDINARY GLAZED MINI BUNDT CAKE

450 calories (1⅔ times the calories), 28 g fat (14 times the fat)

TWO-TONE GLAZE

For this variation, use half regular confectioners' sugar, and half chocolate confectioners' sugar. To each half, whisk in 1 to 2 tablespoons low-fat milk (1%) until it reaches good glazing consistency.

LITTLE CHOCOLATE CROWN CAKES

In place of the white cake batter in this recipe, substitute the chocolate cake batter from The Littlest Angel Cakes, page 88.

only 1 gram of fat!

Can you believe it! Buttermilk, egg whites, and liquid egg substitute will do it every time. Even though the egg substitute is mostly egg whites—and we already have 2 whites in the recipe—it gives the cake a yellow color and makes for a better texture.

The Littlest Angel Cakes

MAKES 6 DIVINE LITTLE ANGELS

PREP: 30 MINUTES

BAKE: AT 350° FOR 12 TO 15 MINUTES

You've heard of angel food cake—well, these are little cakes in the shape of an angel. I must have at least 72,000 angel pins. Everywhere I go, people say, "Richard, you're such an angel. Here, let me pin this angel on you." Sometimes that's tough when you're wearing only a tank top! I believe angels guide our lives, so I decided to create a special miniature angel cake, both white and chocolate, and one that wouldn't spoil our angelic figures. Now when you make these, I want you to get in the right mood. Turn on your CD player and pick one of the following: "Johnny Angel," "Angel in the Morning," or "Angel Baby." And if you have an extra pair of wings . . .

Nonstick vegetable-oil cooking spray

CAKES

½ cup unsweetened cocoa powder

½ cup hot black coffee

1 teaspoon pure vanilla extract or chocolate extract

¼ cup fat-free liquid egg substitute, thawed if frozen

¾ cup superfine sugar

⅔ cup cake flour, <u>sifted</u> twice

4 large egg whites

¼ teaspoon cream of tartar

FROSTING

2 cups confectioners' sugar

3 tablespoons 70% buttermilk-vegetable oil spread

Pinch salt

1 to 1½ tablespoons low-fat milk (1%)

Food coloring

Gold glitter

1. Preheat oven to 350°. Lightly coat 6 individual angel pans (6 ounces each) with nonstick cooking spray.

2. *Make cakes:* In small bowl, whisk together cocoa, hot coffee, and vanilla, until smooth. Let cool.

3. In medium bowl, with mixer on medium-high, beat egg substitute and ½ cup sugar until very thick and volume has tripled. Reduce to low, and alternately beat in flour and cocoa mixture until smooth.

4. In large bowl, with clean beaters, beat whites and cream of tartar on medium-high until soft peaks form. Increase speed to high. Gradually beat in remaining ¼ cup sugar until stiff and glossy peaks form. Fold whites into chocolate batter. Fill pans. Place on baking sheet.

5. Bake in 350° oven until a wooden pick inserted in centers comes out clean, 12 to 15 minutes. Cool cakes in pans on wire racks for 5 minutes. Loosen edges of cakes with small table knife. Invert cakes onto racks, remove pans, and cool completely.

6. *Make frosting:* In medium bowl, combine confectioners' sugar, vegetable oil spread, and salt. Add 1 tablespoon milk. With electric mixer on medium speed, beat until smooth and fluffy. Stir in enough of remaining milk to make good spreading consistency.

7. *To decorate:* Remove ½ cup frosting to small bowl. Leave remaining frosting plain, or tint with food coloring. Tint ½ cup in contrasting color. Spread larger amount over angels. Spoon ½ cup into pastry bag fitted with small writing tip, or into plastic food-storage bag, with ⅛ inch of corner snipped off. Pipe on angels. Sprinkle glitter on for hair.

NUTRIENT VALUE PER MY LITTLEST ANGEL CAKE, WITHOUT FROSTING

173 calories, 6 g protein, 1 g fat (6% fat; 1 g saturated fat), 38 g carbohydrate, 57 mg sodium, 0 mg cholesterol

WITH FROSTING

348 calories, 6 g protein, 7 g fat (17% fat; 2 g saturated fat), 71 g carbohydrate, 195 mg sodium, 0 mg cholesterol

AN ORDINARY FROSTED CHOCOLATE CAKE

602 calories (almost twice the calories), 28 g fat (4 times the fat)

MORE LITTLEST ANGELS

In place of the chocolate batter, substitute the white cake batter from Little Crown Cakes, page 86.

Do you think if you don't eat a pie right away
And it stays in your fridge to get moldy and gray
That, left in this state, it will finally die
And float off to heaven as "Pie in the Sky"?

Well let's just suppose that this sad story's true.
Then here is what I suggest you all do:
Bring in your friends and divide up these wedges,
And remember, no nibbling to neaten the edges.

Divided this way there won't be a chance
Of leftover pie in a heavenly trance.
But if you're alone and your cravings unravel,
Quick, send off your pie for a little sky travel!

Pie in the Sky

My, Oh My! Chocolate Mousse Pie

MAKES 12 SERVINGS

PREP: 30 MINUTES, PLUS CHILLING

BAKE: CRUST AT 350° FOR 5 MINUTES

Like so many of my culinary introductions, I first met a chocolate mousse when I was a child, in a fancy New Orleans hotel, the Roosevelt. Anyway, it was love at first taste, even though I wasn't quite sure what to make of it. I asked where mousse came from. Was there a Mr. Mousse who created it for

Mrs. Mousse, like the great chef who created the fabulous meringue dessert for the Russian ballerina Anna Pavlova? Could I use the leftovers in my hair? No one knew. But I did learn in high school that the word *mousse*, in French, means "foam" or "froth"—chocolate foam, what could be better! Years later, after my long affair with chocolate mousse, I went into my kitchen and created this version, a mousse in a crust, which is so light it practically floats.

CRUST

8 *reduced-fat chocolate graham cracker rectangles*

1 *tablespoon honey*

1 *tablespoon 70% buttermilk-vegetable oil spread, melted*

FILLING

1 *envelope unflavored gelatin*

¼ *cup cold water*

1 *can (12 ounces) evaporated skim milk*

3 *tablespoons unsweetened cocoa powder*

2 *tablespoons granulated sugar*

7 *ounces dark (semisweet) chocolate (European-style bar chocolate), broken into pieces*

2 *teaspoons pure vanilla extract*

2 *cups frozen nonfat nondairy whipped topping, thawed*

1 Preheat oven to 350°.

2 *Make crust:* Break up graham crackers and place in food processor. Process into fine crumbs. Add honey and vegetable oil spread. With on/off motion, pulse until evenly moistened. Turn into 9-inch springform pan. Spread crumbs evenly over bottom of pan and 1½ inches up the sides. Cover with piece of plastic wrap and press crust firmly. Remove plastic.

3 Bake crust in 350° oven for 5 minutes. Transfer pan to wire rack to cool completely.

4 *Make filling:* In small saucepan, sprinkle gelatin over ¼ cup cold water. Let stand for 1 minute, until gelatin softens. Place pan over low heat and stir until gelatin dissolves.

5 In medium saucepan, bring evaporated milk to a boil, stirring occasionally. Stir in cocoa powder, sugar, and chocolate. With wire whisk, mix until smooth. Stir in vanilla and gelatin mixture. Pour into large bowl and cool to room temperature. Refrigerate, stirring every 10 minutes, until mixture thickens and begins to mound, about 30 to 45 minutes. Gently fold in whipped topping. Pour into crust. Refrigerate until set, about 2 hours.

NUTRIENT VALUE PER SERVING OF MY MOUSSE PIE

188 calories, 5 g protein, 7 g fat (32% fat; 4 g saturated fat), 29 g carbohydrate, 107 mg sodium, 1 mg cholesterol

THE USUAL CHOCOLATE MOUSSE PIE

465 calories (almost 2½ time the calories), 37 g fat (more than 5 times the fat)

accessorizing

Use just a small amount of chocolate—½ ounce will do it—for these decorations (no need to cover the entire top of a cake). You'll get a lot of beauty for your calories.

CURLS: Scrape a swivel-bladed vegetable peeler over the edge of a block of chocolate. You'll get better curls if the chocolate is at room temperature—carry it around in your pocket for an hour or two (just kidding!).

LEAVES: Paint melted chocolate onto plant leaves (make sure the leaves are not poisonous), and refrigerate to firm up. Gently peel off the real leaves.

HEARTS: Spoon some melted chocolate into a little pastry bag fitted with a small writing tip, or into a small plastic food-storage bag with ⅛ inch of a corner snipped off. Pipe heart shapes onto a piece of waxed paper. Put in the refrigerator until the chocolate firms up, and then gently remove with a wooden pick or tweezers and arrange on the dessert.

Cinderella Pumpkin Pie

MAKES 10 SERVINGS

PREP: 20 MINUTES

BAKE: CRUST AT 425° FOR 12 TO 15
MINUTES; PIE AT 350° FOR 45 TO 55
MINUTES

The Fairy Godmother waved her wand, and the pumpkin became a gorgeous coach, and the mice . . . we all know the rest. Except most of you probably don't know that after Cinderella left for the Harvest Moon Ball, the Fairy Godmother waved her wand again, and there it was—a gigantic pumpkin. One more wave, and the ugly stepsisters put on their aprons and made 752 pumpkin pies to sell at the church bazaar. But back at the ball, at the stroke of twelve, Cinderella limped down the palace steps, wearing just one glass slipper. There in the road was her coach—a few pieces of pumpkin shell. "My carriage!" Rod Serling peeked around a tree and whispered, "You're in the twilight zone, dear!"

CRUST
¾ cup cake flour
¼ cup all-purpose flour
1 teaspoon granulated sugar
Pinch salt
¼ cup (½ stick) 70% buttermilk-vegetable oil spread, cut into pieces and chilled
2 tablespoons cold water

FILLING
1 can (15 ounces) solid-pack pumpkin puree
1 cup evaporated low-fat milk
½ cup maple syrup
⅓ cup packed light-brown sugar

2 large egg whites
1 large whole egg
1 teaspoon ground cinnamon
½ teaspoon ground ginger
¼ teaspoon ground allspice
Pinch ground cloves
1 teaspoon pure vanilla extract
Pinch salt

1 Place oven rack in lowest position. Preheat oven to 425°.

2 *Make crust:* In medium bowl, stir together both flours, sugar, and salt. With pastry blender, 2 knives used like scissors, or your fingertips, cut in vegetable oil spread until mixture resembles coarse meal. Sprinkle with 2 tablespooons cold water, and toss lightly with fork to moisten. Gather into a ball.

3 On lightly floured waxed paper, roll out dough to 12-inch round (it will be thin). Invert waxed paper with dough into 9-inch pie pan. Peel off waxed paper. Fit dough into bottom and up sides of pan. Crimp edges to form ¼-inch-high border around edge. With fork, prick bottom of crust in several places.

4 Bake on lowest oven rack in 425° oven until very pale gold, 12 to 15 minutes. Transfer to wire rack to cool briefly. Reduce oven temperature to 350°.

5 *Make filling:* In large bowl, whisk together pumpkin puree, milk, syrup, brown sugar, egg whites, whole egg, the spices, vanilla, and salt, until smooth. Pour into pie crust. Carefully return pan to lowest oven rack.

You'll notice that I jazz up this pie with my own spice combo—it's better than what you find in that little spice jar in the supermarket. You can sprinkle this in apple pie, puddings, or over blanched broccoli—really.

6 Bake on lowest oven rack in 350° oven until center is firm, not jiggly, 45 to 55 minutes. Transfer to wire rack to cool.

NUTRIENT VALUE PER SLICE OF MY PIE
174 calories, 4 g protein, 5 g fat (26% fat; 2 g saturated fat), 28 g carbohydrate, 114 mg sodium, 25 mg cholesterol

TRADITIONAL PUMPKIN PIE
286 calories (1½ times the calories), 13 g fat (2½ times the fat)

fat-buster

I've cut back the fat in my pie crust by at least half, as compared with the usual butter- or shortening-filled versions. But this created a problem. Keep in mind, when you reduce the amount of fat in pastry, it gets tough. So here's my solution: I've replaced some of the all-purpose flour with cake flour, which has a finer texture and makes for more tender pastry. You can use this crust in any of your favorite pie recipes.

Lost-in-Boston Cream Pie

MAKES 10 SERVINGS

PREP: 30 MINUTES, PLUS CHILLING

BAKE: AT 350° FOR 30 TO 35 MINUTES

I always look forward to visiting the malls around Boston—Natick, Medford, Framingham, Dedham, Saugus. But I could never find a piece of Boston Cream Pie—it just seemed to be missing. I was doing a radio program in Worcester, and finally I pleaded, "Please, somebody call and tell me where I can find the pie." Someone did, and my prayer was answered. Off I went to the Parker House Hotel in downtown Boston. As I sat in the hotel coffee shop, the waiter came up and said, "You look like Richard Simmons. Are you lost in Boston?" "Bring me a piece of Boston Cream Pie, and then I'll tell you." They had it! And you know what? It's not even a pie, but a cake that looks like a pie. Arturo the waiter even took me back into the kitchen where, encased in plastic, was the leftover piece from the first pie made in 1856. Bostonians do love their history.

VANILLA CUSTARD

⅓ cup granulated sugar

2 tablespoons all-purpose flour

2 tablespoons cornstarch

¼ teaspoon salt

1 large egg

2 cups low-fat milk (1%)

1½ tablespoons 70% buttermilk-vegetable oil spread

1 teaspoon pure vanilla extract

¼ teaspoon orange extract

CAKE

Nonstick vegetable-oil cooking spray

½ cup granulated sugar

3 tablespoons 70% buttermilk-vegetable oil spread, at room temperature

1 large egg yolk

1 teaspoon pure vanilla extract

½ teaspoon orange extract

1 cup cake flour

½ teaspoon baking powder

½ teaspoon salt

½ cup low-fat buttermilk

2 large egg whites

CHOCOLATE GLAZE

2½ tablespoons unsweetened cocoa powder

⅓ cup low-fat sweetened condensed milk

2 tablespoons water

1 **Make vanilla custard:** In medium bowl, stir together sugar, flour, cornstarch, salt, and egg, until blended. In medium, heavy saucepan, heat milk over medium heat until small bubbles appear around edge of pan. Gradually whisk milk into flour mixture. Return all of mixture to saucepan and cook over medium heat, whisking, until thickened and bubbly, 2 to 3 minutes. Reduce heat to low and cook, whisking, another 2 minutes. Remove from heat. Stir in vegetable oil spread and vanilla and orange extracts. Cool slightly. Press waxed paper directly onto surface of custard and refrigerate until firm, several hours or overnight.

2 **Make cake:** Preheat oven to 350°. Coat 8-inch round layer-cake pan with nonstick cooking spray. In

NUTRIENT VALUE
PER SERVING OF MY
BOSTON CREAM PIE

234 calories, 6 g protein, 7 g fat
(26% fat; 2 g saturated fat),
38 g carbohydrate, 288 mg
sodium, 47 mg cholesterol

THE CLASSIC

517 calories (more than twice
the calories), 22 g fat (more than
3 times the fat)

medium bowl, with electric mixer on medium speed, beat sugar and vegetable oil spread, until blended. Beat in egg yolk and vanilla and orange extracts, until smooth. In small bowl, stir together cake flour, baking powder, and salt. Alternately stir flour mixture and buttermilk into egg yolk mixture, beginning and ending with flour, until smooth batter forms.

3 In another medium bowl, with clean beaters, beat egg whites on medium-high until stiff and glossy peaks form. Fold into batter. Spoon batter into prepared pan.

4 Bake in 350° oven until a wooden pick inserted in center comes out clean, 30 to 35 minutes. Cool cake completely in pan on wire rack.

5 *Just before assembling, make glaze:* In small saucepan, stir together cocoa powder, condensed milk, and 2 tablespoons water, until blended. Heat over low heat, stirring constantly, until mixture bubbles and thickens, about 2 minutes. Cook, stirring, 1 minute longer. Remove from heat and cool slightly.

6 *To assemble:* Remove cake from pan. With long serrated knife, cut cake in half horizontally. Place bottom half of cake, cut side up, on cake plate. Spread custard evenly over top. Top with second cake half, cut side down. Spread glaze evenly over top. This can be refrigerated, uncovered, overnight. Also, if custard layer begins to ooze too much, refrigerate. Serve at room temperature or slightly chilled.

Lemon Merenga Pie

MAKES 10 SERVINGS

PREP: 25 MINUTES, PLUS CHILLING

COOK: ABOUT 8 MINUTES

BAKE: CRUST AT 350° FOR 8 MINUTES; PIE
AT 375° FOR 8 MINUTES

There's a small tropical island off the coast of Cuba called Merenga. The islanders, called Merengans, had a national flag, a national bird, and a national plant, but no dish they were famous for. The island was known for its lush lemon groves, so it had to be something with lemons. You guessed it—they created a Lemon Merenga Pie. In the early 1930s, Merengans began to immigrate to New York City, where they worked in restaurants and bakeries making their special pie. One day in a little luncheonette on Grand Street, the cashier was writing out the day's menu on a chalkboard and misspelled a word. And that's how *merenga* became *meringue*.

CRUST

- 8 whole graham cracker rectangles, broken up
- ¼ cup sliced blanched almonds
- 2 tablespoons 70% buttermilk-vegetable oil spread
- 1 tablespoon honey

FILLING

- ½ cup + 2 tablespoons granulated sugar
- ¼ cup cornstarch
- 1½ cups cold water
- ½ cup fat-free liquid egg substitute, thawed if frozen
- 2 teaspoons grated lemon zest
- ¼ cup + 1 tablespoon fresh lemon juice
- 1 tablespoon 70% buttermilk-vegetable oil spread

MERINGUE

- 4 large egg whites
- Pinch salt
- ½ cup granulated sugar

1 Preheat oven to 350°.

2 *Make crust:* In food processor, process graham crackers and almonds together until finely crumbed. Add vegetable oil spread and honey. Pulse with on/off motion until evenly blended. Press crumb mixture over bottom and up sides of 9-inch pie pan.

3 Bake crust in 350° oven until just set and lightly colored, about 8 minutes. Transfer pan to wire rack to cool.

4 *Meanwhile, make filling:* In medium, heavy saucepan, stir together sugar and cornstarch. Stir in 1½ cups cold water until cornstarch dissolves. Cook over medium heat, stirring constantly, until bubbly and thickened, 2 to 3 minutes. Cook, stirring, 2 minutes longer.

5 Pour egg substitute into small bowl. Gradually whisk in one-third of hot mixture. Return egg substitute mixture to saucepan. Cook over low heat, stirring, 3 minutes. Remove from heat. Stir in lemon zest, lemon juice, and vegetable oil spread. Spread filling evenly in pie crust. Cool to lukewarm. Refrigerate, uncovered, until firm and chilled, at least 1 hour.

6 *Just before serving, make meringue:* Preheat oven to 375°. In medium bowl, with electric mixer on medium speed, beat together egg whites and salt, until frothy. Gradually add sugar, 1 tablespoon at a time, and beat until stiff and glossy peaks form. Spread meringue over filling, making sure meringue touches crust all around, sealing completely.

7 Bake in 375° oven until meringue is golden, about 8 minutes. Transfer pan to wire rack to cool.

NUTRIENT VALUE PER SLICE OF MY LEMON MERENGA PIE

209 calories, 4 g protein, 6 g fat (26% fat; 1 g saturated fat), 37 g carbohydrate, 144 mg sodium, 0 mg cholesterol

TRADITIONAL LEMON MERINGUE PIE

395 calories (almost twice the calories), 14 g fat (2⅓ times the fat)

my main squeeze

For this pie you need lemon juice, and it must be fresh. None of that stuff in a bottle. Figure about 2 tablespoons of juice from 1 medium lemon. Do the math—I'll wait. About 3 lemons—did you get that? There's 4 tablespoons in ¼ cup, plus you need another tablespoon, for a total of 5 tablespoons. So that's a little more than 2 lemons, or 3 to be on the safe side. Now here's the trick for getting the most juice out of the lemon: Make sure it's at room temperature. With the lemon on the counter, gently lean on it with the palm of your hand, and roll it around to break up the pulp inside. No, the lemon won't scream! Cut the lemon in half across its middle, and juice away.

Orange You a Gorgeous Tart!

MAKES 10 SERVINGS

PREP: 30 MINUTES, PLUS CHILLING

BAKE: CRUST AT 375° FOR 12 TO 15 MINUTES

What did you call me?! What? This tart will definitely turn heads, it's so beautiful. When I created this recipe, I was trying to recapture the flavor of the orange Creamsicles I had when I was a child in New Orleans. I would eat five of them on the way to school—one for each block.

CRUST

¾ cup cake flour

¼ cup all-purpose flour

1 teaspoon granulated sugar

Pinch salt

¼ cup (½ stick) 70% buttermilk-vegetable oil spread, cut into pieces and chilled

2 tablespoons cold water

FILLING

1 can (14 ounces) fat-free sweetened condensed milk

1 container (8 ounces) low-fat plain yogurt

¼ cup + 2 tablespoons fresh lemon juice

1 tablespoon grated orange zest

1½ teaspoons unflavored gelatin

2 tablespoons cold water

3 large navel oranges

1 teaspoon chopped pistachio nuts, for garnish (optional)

1 Preheat oven to 375°.

2 *Make crust:* In medium bowl, stir together both flours, sugar, and salt. With pastry blender, 2 knives used like scissors, or your fingertips, cut in vegetable oil spread until mixture resembles fine crumbs. Sprinkle with 2 tablespoons cold water and toss lightly with fork to moisten. Gather into ball.

3 On lightly floured waxed paper, roll out dough to 10-inch round. Invert waxed paper with dough into 9-inch tart pan with removable bottom. Peel off waxed paper. Fit dough into bottom and up sides of pan (any broken pieces can be easily patched by hand). Trim edges. With fork, prick bottom of crust in several places.

4 Bake in 375° oven until lightly browned in center, 12 to 15 minutes. Transfer pan to wire rack to cool.

5 *Meanwhile, make filling:* In medium bowl, whisk together sweetened condensed milk, yogurt, lemon juice, and orange zest. In small heatproof bowl, sprinkle gelatin over 2 tablespoons cold water and let stand until softened, 3 minutes. Then set bowl in skillet of simmering water and stir until gelatin completely dissolves. Whisk dissolved gelatin into condensed milk mixture. Pour into tart shell and spread evenly with rubber spatula. Refrigerate until firm, about 1 hour.

6 Peel oranges, removing all bitter white pith. Cut oranges lengthwise in half. Place, flat side down, on cutting surface. Cut crosswise into thin slices. Arrange orange semicircles, slightly overlapping, in concentric rings on top of filling. Just before serving, remove side of tart pan, and sprinkle chopped pistachios over top of tart, if you'd like.

inny or outty?

For a brand-new Chrysler
Prowler, can you name the three
general categories of oranges?
Give up? There are sweet,
loose-skinned, and bitter. Are we
describing oranges, or my friends!
In this tart I use a navel orange,
which is a sweet orange, and
even better, it's seedless, so
there's no sitting for hours with a
hat pin picking out all those little
seeds. How do you spot these in
the supermarket? They have a
gorgeous belly button, or navel,
at one end. It's usually an outty,
but every now and then you'll
find an inny.

Strawberry Fields Tart

MAKES 10 SERVINGS

PREP: 20 MINUTES, PLUS CHILLING

BAKE: CRUST AT 375° FOR 12 TO 15
MINUTES

COOK: ABOUT 5 MINUTES

When I first arrived in California, I discovered a tiny candy store in my neighborhood. In the window was a lady, sitting on a high stool, who dipped the hugest strawberries—they were from another planet— in white chocolate. With a great flourish, she swirled them around, creating a little curlicue on the end, and as she gently laid them on waxed paper to dry, people on the sidewalk gave her a "stemming" ovation. I loved the taste—the combination of the juicy red strawberry with the white chocolate. It was perfection, but the amount of fat from the white chocolate was unbelievable. That flavor combination is the inspiration for this tart, and even though the strawberries are not fully dipped, you'll still applaud the results.

CRUST

½ cup quick-cooking oats

½ cup + 1 tablespoon all-purpose flour

2 tablespoons granulated sugar

¼ teaspoon baking soda

¼ teaspoon salt

¼ cup (½ stick) 70% buttermilk-vegetable oil spread, cut into pieces and chilled

1 tablespoon cold water

2 teaspoons fresh lemon juice

FILLING

1¼ cups evaporated skim milk

1 large egg

¼ cup granulated sugar

1½ tablespoons cornstarch

2½ ounces good-quality white chocolate

1 pound fresh strawberries, stems removed

1 Preheat oven to 375°.

2 *Make crust:* In food processor, process oats until fine crumbs form. Add flour, sugar, baking soda, and salt, and process to mix. Add vegetable oil spread, and pulse with on/off motion until mixture resembles coarse crumbs. Sprinkle with 1 tablespoon cold water and lemon juice, and pulse with on/off motion to moisten. Gather dough into ball.

3 On lightly floured waxed paper, roll out dough to 11-inch round. Invert waxed paper with dough into 9-inch tart pan with removable bottom. Peel off waxed paper and fit dough into bottom and up sides of tart pan. Trim edges. With fork, prick bottom of crust in several places.

4 Bake in 375° oven until lightly browned in center, 12 to 15 minutes. Transfer pan to wire rack to cool.

5 *Make filling:* In large bowl, whisk together ¼ cup evaporated milk, egg, sugar, and cornstarch, until blended. In small, heavy saucepan, heat remaining 1 cup evaporated milk over medium heat until small bubbles appear around edge of pan. Gradually whisk hot milk into egg mixture. Return egg mixture to

saucepan and cook over medium heat, whisking constantly, until mixture thickens, 2 to 3 minutes. Reduce heat to low and cook, whisking, 2 minutes longer. Remove from heat. Chop 2 ounces white chocolate and whisk into hot mixture until smooth. Pour mixture into tart shell, and spread evenly with rubber spatula. Cool slightly. Place in refrigerator and chill completely.

6 Just before serving, cut strawberries in half lengthwise. Arrange strawberry halves decoratively on top of filling. With vegetable peeler, finely shave remaining ½ ounce of white chocolate over tart. Remove side of tart pan.

NUTRIENT VALUE PER SLICE OF MY TART

197 calories, 5 g protein, 7 g fat (31% fat; 3 g saturated fat), 28 g carbohydrate, 173 mg sodium, 24 mg cholesterol

THE USUAL STRAWBERRY TART WITH WHITE CHOCOLATE CUSTARD

364 calories (almost twice the calories), 17 g fat (almost 2½ times the fat)

crusty trickery

What's that nutty taste in the crust? Fooled you! There are no nuts—it's oats. And when the crust gets prebaked, it gets all nutty-tasting. Plus, I added a little lemon juice to jazz up the flavor even more.

Apple-Custard Pie with a Twist

MAKES 10 SERVINGS

PREP: 25 MINUTES

**BAKE: PIE AT 375° FOR 20 MINUTES;
THEN WITH STREUSEL FOR 20 TO 25
MINUTES**

Remember that rhyme? "Apples, peaches, pumpkin pie, you were there and so was I." Well, if you missed it, you can still make this. By now, you've probably figured out I have this thing for custardy desserts—they just make my eyes glaze over. With this apple pie, instead of slicing, I grate, so the taste of apple is everywhere. And if that weren't enough, I top it all off with a crumbly brown sugar-cinnamon mixture. And then there's the twist—no, not Chubby Checker's twist. Mine—a twist of lemon in the filling.

CRUST

¾ cup cake flour

¼ cup all-purpose flour

1 teaspoon granulated sugar

Pinch salt

¼ cup (½ stick) 70% buttermilk-vegetable oil spread,
   cut into pieces and chilled

2 tablespoons cold water

FILLING

3 Golden Delicious apples

1 tablespoon fresh lemon juice

3 tablespoons all-purpose flour

1 large whole egg

1 large egg white

½ cup granulated sugar

½ cup low-fat milk (1%)

¼ cup reduced-fat sour cream

½ teaspoon grated lemon zest

Pinch salt

STREUSEL

¼ cup quick-cooking oats

¼ cup all-purpose flour

2 tablespoons light-brown sugar

¼ teaspoon ground cinnamon

Pinch salt

1 tablespoon 70% buttermilk-vegetable oil spread,
   chilled

About 1 tablespoon water

1 Preheat oven to 375°.

2 *Make crust:* In medium bowl, stir together both flours, sugar, and salt. With pastry blender, 2 knives held like scissors, or your fingertips, cut in vegetable oil spread until mixture resembles fine crumbs. Sprinkle with 2 tablespoons cold water and toss lightly with fork to moisten. Gather into ball.

3 On lightly floured waxed paper, roll out dough to 10½-inch round (dough will be thin). Invert waxed paper with dough into 9-inch pie pan. Peel off waxed paper. Fit dough into bottom and up sides of pan. Trim edges. Refrigerate while making filling.

4 *Make filling:* Peel and coarsely grate apples to make 3 cups. Place in fine-mesh sieve and press to remove excess liquid. In medium bowl, toss grated apple with lemon juice. Then mix in 1 tablespoon flour. In another medium bowl, mix together remaining 2 tablespoons flour, whole egg, egg white, sugar, milk, sour cream, lemon zest, and salt, until blended. Stir in apple mixture. Spread filling evenly in pie crust.

5 Bake in 375° oven for 20 minutes.

6 *Meanwhile, make streusel:* In small bowl, stir together oats, flour, brown sugar, cinnamon, and salt. With your fingertips, work in vegetable oil spread by pinching and rubbing until mixture resembles fine crumbs and holds together when pressed. Sprinkle with about 1 tablespoon water and toss lightly with fork to moisten. After pie has baked for 20 minutes, sprinkle streusel over filling.

7 Bake in 375° oven until center is firm and slightly puffed, for another 20 to 25 minutes. Transfer to wire rack to cool slightly. Serve warm or at room temperature.

NUTRIENT VALUE PER SERVING OF
MY APPLE PIE

205 calories, 4 g protein, 7 g fat (28% fat; 2 g saturated fat), 33 g carbohydrate, 109 mg sodium, 24 mg cholesterol

THE CLASSIC APPLE PIE

390 calories (almost twice the calories), 13 g fat (1¾ times the fat)

My Little Tartlets

MAKES 8 TARTLETS

PREP: 30 MINUTES, PLUS CHILLING

BAKE: AT 375° FOR 10 TO 12 MINUTES

In New Orleans there was a pastry shop on Royal Street that was my second home. It was called the Four Seasons, and behind the counter was Evelyn, a smiling lady. They had the most gorgeous fruit tarts, big ones and small ones, with a thick custard filling and a shiny glaze so bright you had to wear sunglasses. At certain times of the day Evelyn would put fresh tarts in the display cases, and I knew her schedule like clockwork. I'd be there waiting, nose pressed against the window. She'd look up, see me, and nod. I dedicate my tartlets to Evelyn.

CRUST

¾ cup all-purpose flour

¾ cup cake flour

1½ teaspoons granulated sugar

Pinch salt

6 tablespoons (¾ stick) 70% buttermilk-vegetable oil spread, cut into pieces and chilled

3 tablespoons cold water + 1 to 2 teaspoons more as needed

FILLING

3 ounces reduced-fat cream cheese

6 tablespoons reduced-fat ricotta cheese

3 tablespoons confectioners' sugar

½ teaspoon pure vanilla extract

GLAZE AND TOPPING

2 tablespoons seedless raspberry jam

1 teaspoon orange liqueur or orange juice

2½ cups mixed sliced fresh fruit and berries

1 *Make crust:* In medium bowl, stir together both flours, sugar, and salt. With pastry blender, 2 knives held like scissors, or your fingertips, cut in vegetable oil spread until mixture resembles fine crumbs. Sprinkle 3 tablespoons cold water over mixture and toss with fork to moisten. Gather dough into a ball, adding another 1 to 2 teaspoons water if necessary for dough to hold together. Flatten into disk. Cover in plastic wrap, and refrigerate at least 20 minutes.

2 *Make filling:* In small bowl, with electric mixer on medium speed, beat cream cheese until fluffy. With rubber spatula, press ricotta cheese through sieve into cream cheese. Add confectioners' sugar and vanilla, and beat until blended. Cover and refrigerate at least 2 hours to thicken slightly.

3 Place oven rack in upper third of oven. Preheat oven to 375°.

4 Divide dough into 8 equal pieces. On floured surface, roll one piece of dough into 5-inch round. Fit into Texas-size (3½ × 1¾ inches) or jumbo muffin-pan cup. Repeat with remaining pieces of dough and 7 more muffin-pan cups. Prick bottoms with fork.

5 Bake in upper third of 375° oven until golden, 10 to 12 minutes. Transfer to wire rack to cool. Remove from pans.

6 *Make glaze:* In small saucepan, combine jam and liqueur or orange juice over low heat, stirring, until melted. Let cool slightly.

7 *To assemble:* Spoon filling into shells. Arrange fruit on top. Brush with glaze. Serve, or chill until serving.

cornucopia of fruit

I've filled these tartlets with fresh figs, peaches, strawberries, blueberries, and grapes. But follow your own whim—use whatever fruit is in season.

NUTRIENT VALUE PER MY TARTLET
232 calories, 5 g protein, 10 g fat (38% fat; 3 g saturated fat), 29 g carbohydrate, 136 mg sodium, 8 mg cholesterol

USUAL CUSTARD FRUIT TARTLET
564 calories (almost 2½ times the calories), 29 g fat (almost 3 times the fat)

Yes, We Have a Banana Cream Pie

MAKES 10 SERVINGS

PREP: 15 MINUTES, PLUS CHILLING

BAKE: CRUST AT 400° FOR 18 MINUTES

COOK: ABOUT 6 MINUTES

Every week my parents used to take me to Morrison's Cafeteria. Imagine me in a cafeteria with all those choices? Fortunately, they made me leave my wagon at the door. At Morrison's, the desserts were always first in the line, and the very first dessert was always banana cream pie. Even before I knew bananas had lots of vitamin C and potassium, I loved them. But it wasn't until years later that I discovered that when you eat out, dessert is not the first course. I always thought that if the French could end a meal with a salad, why not start with a dessert?

CRUST

½ cup all-purpose flour

½ cup cake flour

1 teaspoon granulated sugar

Pinch salt

¼ cup (½ stick) 70% buttermilk-vegetable oil spread, cut into pieces and chilled

2 tablespoons cold water, or as needed

FILLING

¼ cup + 2 tablespoons packed light-brown sugar

1 tablespoon all-purpose flour

1 tablespoon cornstarch

1¼ cups low-fat milk (1%)

½ cup fat-free liquid egg substitute, thawed if frozen

1 tablespoon 70% buttermilk-vegetable oil spread

3 ripe medium-size bananas

1 tablespoon water mixed with 2 teaspoons fresh lemon juice

1 cup frozen nonfat nondairy whipped topping, thawed

1 *Make crust:* In medium bowl, stir together both flours, sugar, and salt. With pastry blender, 2 knives held like scissors, or your fingertips, cut in vegetable oil spread until mixture resembles fine crumbs. Sprinkle 2 tablespoons cold water over mixture and toss lightly with fork to moisten. Gather dough into ball, adding another 1 to 2 teaspoons of water if necessary for dough to hold together. On lightly floured waxed paper, roll out dough to 11-inch round (it will be thin). Invert waxed paper with dough into 9-inch pie pan. Peel off waxed paper. Fit dough into bottom and up sides of pan. Pinch together excess dough along rim of pan to make an even edge. Refrigerate at least 20 minutes.

2 Place oven rack in upper third of oven. Preheat oven to 400°. With fork, prick bottom of crust in several places. Line crust with aluminum foil. Fill with pie weights or dried beans.

3 Bake in upper third of 400° oven until very lightly browned all over, about 18 minutes. Remove foil with weights. Transfer pan to wire rack to cool.

4 *Meanwhile, make filling:* In medium, heavy saucepan, stir together brown sugar, flour, and cornstarch. Stir in ¼ cup milk until blended. Add remaining 1 cup milk and heat mixture to boiling over medium heat, stirring constantly. Reduce heat and cook at low boil, stirring, 2 minutes. Pour egg substitute into small bowl. Gradually whisk in

anti-sogging device

I bake this crust blind—no, I don't put a blindfold on. I line the pie shell with aluminum foil and then weight it down with little pie weights or dried beans. This prevents the crust from puffing up and ensures a thoroughly baked crust that will remain crisp when the custardy filling is added. Also, baking in the upper third of the oven, which is the hottest part, means a crisper crust.

about half of hot milk mixture. Return all of mixture to saucepan and cook over low heat, stirring, 2 minutes. Remove from heat and stir in vegetable oil spread.

5 *To assemble:* Peel bananas and slice into ¼-inch-thick rounds. In medium bowl, toss banana slices with lemon juice mixture. Arrange half the slices over bottom of pie crust, overlapping if necessary. Top with hot filling, spreading evenly. Arrange remaining banana slices in a single layer on top of

filling. Refrigerate pie, uncovered, until chilled and firm, at least 1 hour. Just before serving, decorate top with piped or dolloped whipped topping.

NUTRIENT VALUE PER SLICE OF
MY BANANA CREAM PIE
170 calories, 4 g protein, 6 g fat (32% fat; 1 g saturated fat), 27 g carbohydrate, 99 mg sodium, 1 mg cholesterol
TRADITIONAL BANANA CREAM PIE
410 calories (almost 2½ times the calories), 15 g fat (2½ times the fat)

Peachy Cream Pie

MAKES 10 SERVINGS

PREP: 20 MINUTES

BAKE: AT 375° FOR 15 MINUTES; THEN AT 350° FOR 35 TO 40 MINUTES

This is so yummy. Take a taste and you'll be fooled. It's almost like a creamy soufflé—so dreamy. But there wasn't even a carton of cream in the house, anywhere, when I created this. You'll have to read the recipe to see how I do it. You know, I don't like to say it, but this is the kind of custardy dessert I love to squeeze between my front teeth, and then—oh, c'mon, don't tell me you haven't done that.

CRUST

¾ cup cake flour

¼ cup all-purpose flour

1 teaspoon granulated sugar

Pinch salt

¼ cup (½ stick) 70% buttermilk-vegetable oil spread, cut into pieces and chilled

2 tablespoons cold water

FILLING

1¼ pounds fresh ripe peaches, pitted and sliced

¼ cup all-purpose flour

¼ cup + plus 2 teaspoons granulated sugar

1 large whole egg

½ cup low-fat buttermilk

⅓ cup peach jam

1 teaspoon pure vanilla extract

Pinch salt

2 large egg whites

1. *Make crust:* In medium bowl, stir together both flours, sugar, and salt. With pastry blender, 2 knives held like scissors, or your fingertips, cut in vegetable oil spread until mixture resembles fine crumbs. Sprinkle with 2 tablespoons cold water, and toss lightly with fork to moisten. Gather into ball.

2. On lightly floured waxed paper, roll out dough to 10½-inch round (dough will be thin). Invert waxed paper with dough into 9-inch pie plate. Peel off waxed paper and fit dough into bottom and up sides of plate. Trim edges and crimp. Refrigerate while preparing filling.

3. Place oven rack in lowest position. Preheat oven to 375°.

4. *Make filling:* In large bowl, toss peaches with 1 tablespoon flour. In medium bowl, stir together remaining 3 tablespoons flour and the ¼ cup sugar. Whisk in whole egg, buttermilk, jam, vanilla, and salt, until blended. Stir into peach mixture.

5. In clean medium bowl, with electric mixer on medium speed, beat egg whites until frothy. Add remaining 2 teaspoons sugar and beat until soft peaks form. Fold into peach mixture. Spread filling in pie crust.

6. Bake on lowest rack in 375° oven for 15 minutes. Reduce oven temperature to 350° and bake until puffed and browned, and center is firm, another 35 to 40 minutes. Transfer pie plate to wire rack to cool slightly. Serve warm or at room temperature.

NUTRIENT VALUE
PER SLICE OF MY
PEACH PIE

173 calories, 4 g protein,
5 g fat (26% fat; 1 g saturated fat),
29 g carbohydrate, 97 mg
sodium, 22 mg cholesterol

TRADITIONAL PEACH
CUSTARD PIE

266 calories (more than 1½ times
the calories), 11 g fat (more than
twice the fat)

sacred fat

Did you spot it? There's one
whole egg in the filling. But then
my trick is to turn the flavor to
quadraphonic by adding
practically fat-free buttermilk.

A Tisket, a Tasket, a Mini Pear Basket

MAKES 6 INDIVIDUAL BASKETS

PREP: 20 MINUTES

BAKE: PHYLLO BASKETS AT 350° FOR
    15 MINUTES

COOK: ABOUT 25 MINUTES

Every fancy restaurant you go to and every cookbook you open, there it is—this little poached pear, naked, for the all the world to see. Sometimes it's covered in a blushing berry sauce, but it's still naked. There's nothing worse than an embarrassed pear. Let me help that pear, I thought. So I created this delicious, flaky basket, and nestled pear slices in it so they could arrive at the table properly dressed.

PHYLLO BASKETS

Nonstick butter-flavored cooking spray
6 sheets (17 × 12 inches) frozen phyllo dough, thawed according to package directions

FILLING

2 tablespoons chopped walnuts
1 tablespoon butter
4 ripe large pears, peeled, halved, cored, and thinly sliced crosswise
3 tablespoons light-brown sugar
⅓ cup golden raisins
6 tablespoons nonfat plain yogurt, reduced-fat sour cream, or frozen yogurt (optional)

1 Preheat oven to 350°. Lightly coat six 4½-inch glass baking dishes (12 ounces each) or tart pans with nonstick cooking spray. Place phyllo on clean, dry surface. Cover lightly with waxed paper and then with a slightly dampened towel, to prevent drying out.

2 *Make phyllo baskets:* Place sheet of waxed paper on work surface, and lift 1 sheet of phyllo onto waxed paper. Lightly coat with nonstick cooking spray. With remaining 5 sheets, repeat layering and coating with spray. Using sharp knife or pizza wheel cutter, cut stack of phyllo lengthwise in half, and then crosswise into thirds to make 6 equal rectangles. For each basket, place 2 pieces of phyllo from one rectangle in baking dish or tart pan. Separate and place next 2 pieces on top, rotating about 30° to create an uneven edge. Repeat with last 2 pieces. With tip of knife, pierce bottoms in several places.

3 Bake in 350° oven until golden, about 15 minutes. Transfer baskets from dishes to wire rack to cool.

4 *Make filling:* Heat large, nonstick skillet over medium heat. Add walnuts and toast, shaking pan occasionally, until golden and fragrant, 3 to 5 minutes. Remove walnuts to plate and wipe out skillet.

5 In same skillet, heat butter until melted. Add pears and brown sugar and cook, stirring occasionally, until sugar is just slightly syrupy and pears are ten-

der, about 20 minutes. During last 5 minutes of cooking, sprinkle with raisins. Remove from heat and cool slightly.

6 Fill each phyllo basket with slightly rounded ¼ cup warm pear mixture. Sprinkle each with 1 teaspoon walnuts. Serve warm, topped with yogurt, sour cream, or frozen yogurt, if desired.

NUTRIENT VALUE PER SERVING MY PEAR BASKET

217 calories, 3 g protein, 5 g fat (20% fat; 2g saturated fat), 43 g carbohydrate, 95 mg sodium, 5 mg cholesterol

THE USUAL BUTTERY PEAR TART

298 calories (1⅓ times the calories), 15 g fat (3 times the fat)

I'm not much good at sledding
Or at skiing down a hill.

Glaciers give me goosebumps
And of snow I've had my fill.

But what really warms my taste buds
Is behind my freezer door.

If you peek around my shoulder,
You can see what is in store:

A myriad of flavors
That always cause a thrill,

In sweetened pastel colors
I present the great "Big Chill."

The Big Chill

The Melon Trio

PREP: 15 MINUTES, PLUS CHILLING
AND FREEZING

You've heard of the Four Tops, the Andrews Sisters, the Supremes, the Pips. Well, this is the Melon Trio. No, you don't need to sing for your dessert—all you have to do is make it. These are three melons you've had all your life, and now I've transformed them into something even better than a snow cone. You remember the snow cone, along with the Kingston Trio, the Temptations, and the Jackson Five. You can create just one of these granitas, or all three by making the recipe three times, using a different melon for each.

2½ pounds ripe melon (honeydew, cantaloupe, or watermelon), seeds removed, flesh cut into chunks
3 tablespoons superfine sugar
3 tablespoons fresh lemon or lime juice

1 Chill 13 × 9 × 2-inch nonaluminum or other nonreactive metal baking pan in freezer, about 30 minutes.

2 In blender or food processor, place chunks of one type of melon. Puree, and measure out 2 cups into medium bowl. (Save any remaining puree for cold soups, drinks, or another batch of granita.) Into puree, stir sugar and lemon or lime juice. Refrigerate until very cold.

3 Pour chilled melon mixture into chilled metal pan. Freeze until ice crystals form around edges, about 30 minutes. With a fork, stir edges of ice into rest of mixture to evenly incorporate. Continue to freeze, stirring every 30 minutes, until all the liquid freezes completely, about 3 hours total.

4 Spoon into bowls and serve, or scrape into airtight container and store in freezer. If serving from freezer, make sure to let granita soften in refrigerator 20 to 30 minutes so it's not rock hard.

NUTRIENT VALUE PER SERVING OF
MY GRANITA

91 calories, 1 g protein, 0 g fat (0% fat; 0 g saturated fat), 24 g carbohydrate, 19 mg sodium, 0 mg cholesterol

ICE CREAM

150 calories (more than 1½ times the calories), 8 g fat (compared to 0 fat)

the iced dessert cometh

Besides granitas (see Is a Granita a Car?, page 120) there are other frozen tempters:

SORBET is made from a fruit puree or juice, plus sugar—I like using superfine because it dissolves quickly and easily—and water. The texture of sorbet is smoother than its coarser cousin, granita. At one time, egg whites were mixed in to bind the ice crystals together for a firmer, smoother texture. Since the use of raw egg whites is now discouraged for safety reasons, it's best to use an ice-cream maker to get the same smooth texture.

SHERBET is a combination of milk, sugar, and fruit flavor. It's lighter than regular ice cream and richer than a sorbet or granita.

Very Nice Ice

MAKES 10 SERVINGS

*I*ces and ice creams—who would have thought they came from China? But it's true. High up in the Quinqling mountains, a little boy named Li Po figured out how to flavor snow, and the rest is history, ending with two guys in Vermont. I've never met Miss Elizabeth Taylor, but if I ever did, I would make her this dessert, because it's her color—the deepest, most passionate purple.

2 cups fresh or frozen dry-pack raspberries, thawed
1 cup fresh or frozen dry-pack blueberries, thawed
½ cup light corn syrup
½ cup water
¼ cup honey*

1 Chill 13 × 9 × 2-inch nonaluminum or other nonreactive metal baking pan in freezer, about 30 minutes.

2 In blender or food processor, combine raspberries, blueberries, corn syrup, ½ cup water, and honey. Process until smooth. Strain mixture through fine-mesh sieve set over bowl to remove seeds. Pour into chilled metal pan and place in freezer. Every 2 hours, with a fork, stir edges of ice into rest of mixture to evenly incorporate and until evenly crystallized, about 6 hours.

3 Scoop into bowls and serve, or scrape into airtight container and store in freezer. For smoother texture, scrape into food processor. Process just until smooth and serve immediately.

*Note: If you really like the taste of honey, increase honey to ½ cup and reduce amount of corn syrup to ¼ cup.

NUTRIENT VALUE PER SERVING OF MY ICE
92 calories, 0 g protein, 0.19 g fat (2% fat; 0 g saturated fat), 24 g carbohydrate, 21 mg sodium, 0 g cholesterol
BERRY ICE CREAM
150 calories (more than 1½ times the calories), 8 g fat (more than 42 times the fat)

NUTRIENT VALUE
PER MY SUNDAE
253 calories, 6 g protein, 9 g fat
(32% fat; 1 g saturated fat),
40 g carbohydrate, 69 mg sodium,
1 mg cholesterol
TRADITIONAL SUNDAE
506 calories (twice the calories),
12 g fat (1⅓ times the fat)

Five-Minute Sundae

MAKES 1 SERVING

PREP: 5 MINUTES

Got five minutes? Want to make a Sunday? Or a Monday . . . Do you know the story behind the Sundae? In the late 1800s, some very strange people banned drinking carbonated soda on Sunday, including ice cream sodas. All those fizzy bubbles made people too crazy. Well, a boy named Ben decided to have his ice cream on Sunday and eat it, too. He created a "dry" soda and named it—Sundae.

¼ cup nonfat chocolate sorbet
1 tablespoon nonfat chocolate syrup
¼ cup nonfat vanilla frozen yogurt
1 tablespoon nonfat chocolate syrup
2 tablespoons chopped almonds, toasted
Frozen nonfat nondairy whipped topping, thawed, and chopped nuts and syrup, for garnish (optional)

In dessert glass, layer above ingredients in order given. That's it!

Pink Ice Granita

MAKES 6 SERVINGS

PREP: 15 MINUTES, PLUS CHILLING AND FREEZING

Grapefruit are always getting a bum rap. First, there was the broiled grapefruit, looking all wrinkled and tired, in desperate need of a Florida vacation. Then there was the grapefruit diet, where you had to stare at a grapefruit half before each meal. And we all remember when James Cagney pushed a grapefruit half into a woman's face in *Hard to Handle*, 1933. I wanted to take grapefruit to a new plane, so I created this jewel of a dessert.

2 cups fresh grapefruit juice, preferably from ruby red grapefruit (about 2 grapefruit)

¼ cup superfine sugar

2 tablespoons fresh lemon juice

1. Chill 13 × 9 × 2-inch nonaluminum or other nonreactive metal baking pan in freezer, about 30 minutes.

2. In medium bowl, stir together grapefruit juice, sugar, and lemon juice. Refrigerate until very cold.

3. Pour chilled grapefruit mixture into chilled baking pan. Freeze until ice crystals form around edges, about 30 minutes. With a fork, stir edges of ice into rest of mixture to evenly incorporate. Continue to freeze, stirring every 30 minutes, until all the liquid freezes completely, about 3 hours total.

4. Spoon into bowls or hollowed-out orange halves and serve, or scrape into airtight container and store in freezer. If serving from freezer, make sure to let granita soften in refrigerator 20 to 30 minutes so it's not rock hard.

NUTRIENT VALUE PER SERVING OF MY GRANITA

63 calories, 0 g protein, 0 g fat (0% fat; 0 g saturated fat), 16 g carbohydrate, 1 mg sodium, 0 mg cholesterol

ICE CREAM

150 calories (more than 2¼ times the calories), 8 g fat (compared to 0 fat)

is a granita a car?

No, a granita [grah-NEE-ta] is an ice, with absolutely no fat. The French call it a *granité* (grah-nee-TAY) and the Italians, a *granita* (grah-NEE-tah). They're easy to make. Just mix together water, sugar, and a flavoring, and freeze it. To serve, get out your castanets.

Pink-and-White Velvet Semifreddo

MAKES 12 SERVINGS

PREP: 30 MINUTES, PLUS FREEZING, AND CHILLING

I know you're looking at the word "semifreddo" and thinking . . . Stop it! Just stop it! This is not a recipe for fettuccine alfredo. Think _semi_freddo. This is a beautiful Italian dessert, half frozen—that's what _semifreddo_ means in Italian. I had my first one in Venice, and I've never been the same. There I was, sitting in an outdoor cafe in the Piazza San Marco, dipping my spoon into the velvety layers of half-frozen cream. Out of nowhere there swooped down seventy-two pigeons—I was in the middle of an Alfred Hitchcock movie. Those birds carried away half of my semifreddo. So the lesson I learned in Venice is: Eat your semifreddo indoors.

2 cups low-fat (1%) cottage cheese
⅓ cup confectioners' sugar
½ cup granulated sugar
¼ cup water
5 large egg whites
1¼ teaspoons pure vanilla extract
¾ cup frozen strawberries in syrup, partially thawed
1 tablespoon seedless raspberry jam
Fresh raspberries, for garnish (optional)

1. Line 9 × 5 × 3-inch nonaluminum or other nonreactive metal loaf pan with plastic wrap, leaving 3-inch overhang. Place in freezer.

2. In blender or food processor, working in 2 batches, puree together cottage cheese and confectioners' sugar until smooth. Set aside.

3. In small saucepan, stir together granulated sugar and ¼ cup water. In large bowl, with electric mixer on medium-high speed, beat egg whites until firm peaks form. Over medium heat, stirring, bring sugar-water mixture to a boil, and then boil for 2 minutes. With mixer on low speed, gradually pour sugar syrup into whites and beat until well combined. Continue beating until cool. Beat in vanilla. Gradually beat in cottage cheese mixture.

4. In blender or food processor, combine strawberries (including syrup) and jam, and puree until smooth. Transfer to medium bowl. Fold one-third of cottage cheese mixture into berry mixture.

5. Remove pan from freezer. Into bottom of pan, spoon 1¼ cups of berry mixture, making level and smooth with back of spoon. Layer on 1¾ cups of cottage cheese mixture. Repeat layering with remaining berry mixture and cottage cheese mixture. Cover top with plastic-wrap overhang.

6. Freeze until set, about 4 hours.

7. Place loaf in refrigerator 30 minutes before serving. Invert onto platter. Remove pan and peel off plastic wrap. Cut crosswise into 12 slices and serve. Garnish with raspberries, if you'd like.

NUTRIENT VALUE PER SERVING OF MY SEMIFREDDO
95 calories, 6 g protein, 1 g fat (5% fat; 0 g saturated fat), 16 g carbohydrate, 177 mg sodium, 2 mg cholesterol

TRADITIONAL SEMIFREDDO
360 calories (almost 3¾ times the calories), 27 g fat (27 times the fat)

Casa Blanca Cake

MAKES 12 SERVINGS

PREP: 1 HOUR, PLUS FREEZING

No, I'm not doing a remake of *Casablanca* with penguins. But this is the prettiest white house you'll ever see. I actually modeled it after an igloo. The first time I photographed this, I used live penguins, but they ate the cake.

IGLOO

1 package (10 ounces) frozen strawberries in syrup, partially thawed

¼ teaspoon orange extract

1 pint fat-free vanilla frozen yogurt, softened

⅓ cup granulated sugar

¼ cup water

1 bag (12 ounces) frozen dry-pack blueberries, partially thawed

MERINGUE-COCONUT TOPPING

2 tablespoons powdered egg whites

6 tablespoons warm water

⅔ cup granulated sugar

Sweetened flaked coconut, for dusting outside (optional)

1 Line inside of 1½-quart bowl with plastic wrap.

2 *Make igloo:* In food processor, combine strawberries (including syrup) and orange extract. Process until pureed. Scrape mixture into bottom of prepared bowl. Spread, making level and smooth on top. Freeze until almost firm, about 1 hour.

3 In small bowl, reserve ½ cup softened frozen yogurt. Place in freezer until ready to use. Spread remaining frozen yogurt in even layer on top of strawberry layer. Freeze until almost firm, about 1 hour.

4 In small saucepan, combine sugar and ¼ cup water. Heat over medium heat, stirring, until sugar is completely dissolved. Remove from heat.

5 Wipe processor clean. In processor, place reserved frozen yogurt and the blueberries. With machine running, add sugar-water mixture and process until pureed. Spread in even layer over frozen yogurt layer. Cover and freeze at least 6 hours, or overnight.

6 Just before serving, invert igloo onto serving platter and place in freezer. *Make topping:* In medium bowl, gently whisk together powdered egg whites and 6 tablespoons warm water until whites are completely dissolved, about 2 minutes. With electric mixer on medium speed, beat until foamy. Increase speed to medium-high and continue beating, adding sugar, 2 tablespoons at a time, until peaks are stiff and glossy, about 6 minutes. Spread meringue mixture all over igloo to cover completely. Lightly sprinkle outside of igloo with coconut, if desired. Keep frozen until ready to serve. *Tip:* For easier slicing, transfer igloo to refrigerator to soften for 15 to 20 minutes before serving.

NUTRIENT VALUE PER SERVING OF MY CASA BLANCA CAKE

133 calories, 3 g protein, 0 g fat (0 % fat; 0 g saturated fat), 31 g carbohydrate, 35 mg sodium, 1 mg cholesterol

TRADITIONAL ICE CREAM CAKE

496 calories (3¼ times the calories), 32 g fat (compared to 0 fat)

Meringue "Ice Cream" Sandwiches

MAKES 10 MERINGUE SANDWICHES

PREP: 30 MINUTES, PLUS STANDING

BAKE: AT 225° FOR 1 HOUR

They were like shrines on street corners in towns across America—and I was always happy to worship at Our Lady of the Refrigerator Cart. There you could buy these huge ice cream hockey pucks sandwiched between two chocolate cookies. I loved them. Over the years I've experimented with my own ice cream sandwich, and now I have it. Amen! I use almond meringues for the cookies. I've always liked foods that dress up as sandwiches—maybe because it lets you eat and walk at the same time.

3 large egg whites, at room temperature
⅛ teaspoon salt
¾ cup granulated sugar
½ teaspoon pure vanilla extract
⅓ cup sliced blanched almonds
1 pint peach, cherry-vanilla, or raspberry-vanilla swirl frozen yogurt or peach sorbet, slightly softened

1 Preheat oven to 225°. Line 2 large baking sheets with parchment paper or aluminum foil.

2 In large bowl, with electric mixer on medium speed, beat egg whites and salt, until foamy. Gradually beat in 6 tablespoons sugar, 1 tablespoon at a time, until stiff and glossy peaks form. Beat in vanilla. With rubber spatula, fold in remaining 6 tablespoons sugar.

3 Spoon mixture into large pastry bag without tip. Onto prepared baking sheet, pipe meringue into 20 mounds, spacing 3 inches apart. With small metal spatula, flatten mounds into 2½-inch rounds. Sprinkle with almonds.

4 Bake in 225° oven until set and dry, about 1 hour. Turn oven off. Let stand 30 minutes in turned-off oven. Transfer to wire rack to cool.

5 Spread 3 tablespoons frozen yogurt or sorbet onto flat side of one meringue. Top with second meringue. Repeat with remaining frozen yogurt (or sorbet) and meringues. Serve immediately.

NUTRIENT VALUE PER MY MERINGUE SANDWICH

110 calories, 2 g protein, 2 g fat (13% fat; 0 g saturated fat), 22 g carbohydrate, 62 mg sodium, 0 mg cholesterol

HOCKEY-PUCK ICE CREAM SANDWICH

332 calories (3 times the calories), 13 g fat (6½ times the fat)

SPEEDY TREAT

The meringues can be made ahead and stored in an airtight container in a dry place for up to several days. Assemble sandwiches with yogurt for a spur-of-the-moment treat.

Pink-Tie-Only Frozen Soufflé

MAKES 10 SERVINGS

PREP: 20 MINUTES, PLUS CHILLING AND FREEZING

You've heard of black-tie affairs and white-tie galas. Now let me introduce you to the pink-tie soufflé, to be made for only the poshest events. This is so beautiful, I've seen its chilling elegance cause a crowd to gasp. (When I made this once in Paris, a model asked to borrow it to wear as a hat in a fashion show! I told her this is not a sombrero, it's a soufflé.)

½ cup water

1 envelope unflavored gelatin

⅔ cup granulated sugar

1 package (12 ounces) dry-pack frozen raspberries, thawed

3 cups drained, canned sliced peaches in juice, no sugar added

½ cup peach jam

¼ teaspoon almond extract

¼ teaspoon salt

2 tablespoons powdered egg whites

6 tablespoons warm water

1 cup frozen reduced-fat nondairy whipped topping, thawed

Sliced peaches and raspberries, for garnish (optional)

1 Make soufflé collar by cutting piece of waxed paper long enough to go around 1½-quart (3-inch-deep) soufflé dish and to overlap slightly. Fold waxed paper lengthwise in half. Wrap collar around outside of dish, extending about 2 inches above rim. Pull paper tight so filling cannot run down between paper and side of dish. Secure collar with tape.

2 Into small saucepan, pour ½ cup water. Sprinkle gelatin over top. Let stand to soften, 5 minutes. Stir in sugar. Heat over medium heat, stirring, just until gelatin and sugar are dissolved, about 3 minutes; do not let boil. Remove from heat.

3 In food processor, puree raspberries. With rubber spatula, press raspberries through fine-mesh sieve to remove seeds. Return raspberries to processor. Add canned peaches, jam, almond extract, salt, and gelatin mixture. Process to puree. Scrape into large bowl. Refrigerate, stirring, until mixture mounds when dropped from spoon, about 2 hours.

4 In medium bowl, whisk together powdered egg whites and 6 tablespoons warm water until whites are completely dissolved, about 2 minutes. With electric mixer on medium speed, beat until firm peaks form.

5 Gently fold whites into raspberry mixture until no white streaks remain. Fold in whipped topping. Spoon into prepared soufflé dish, smoothing top.

6 Freeze until firm, about 3 hours.

7 To serve, place in refrigerator for 15 to 20 minutes to soften slightly. Remove collar. Garnish with peach slices and raspberries, if you'd like.

NUTRIENT VALUE PER SERVING OF MY SOUFFLÉ

163 calories, 2 g protein, 1 g fat (6% fat; 1 g saturated fat), 38 g carbohydrate, 80 mg sodium, 0 mg cholesterol

A SOUFFLÉ WITH WHOLE EGGS

326 calories (twice the calories), 19 g fat (19 times the fat)

Puddin' eaten cold and plain
Or puddin' eaten glitzy,
Puddin' eaten out or in
Is always somewhat Ritzy.

I've loved puddin' all my life.
You want the honest truth?
I ate puddin' way before
I even grew a tooth.

Puddin' is a perfect food
For people of all ages.
So if you want a puddin' fix,
Then simply flip these pages.

Puddin' on the Ritz

Snow White Coconut Rice Pudding

MAKES 8 SERVINGS

PREP: 5 MINUTES

COOK: 45 TO 50 MINUTES

This pudding is so pure, so white. About halfway through the classic movie, there's a scene where Snow White is making lunch for the Seven Dwarfs. Look carefully—you'll see the pudding on the table.

2 cups water

1 cup long-grain white rice (not converted)

¼ teaspoon salt

3 to 3½ cups low-fat milk (1%)

½ cup granulated sugar

¼ cup sweetened shredded coconut

2 teaspoons pure vanilla extract

SAUCE

1 package (10 ounces) frozen raspberries in syrup, thawed

1. In 3-quart saucepan, bring 2 cups water to a boil. Add rice and salt. Reduce heat. Simmer, covered, until rice is tender and water is absorbed, 15 to 20 minutes.

2. Add 3 cups milk and sugar. Simmer, uncovered, stirring often with heatproof spatula, until thickened and rice is very tender, 30 minutes. Remove from heat. Add coconut and vanilla. Pour into bowl.

3. Let pudding cool slightly. Serve warm, or refrigerate to serve cold. If serving cold, stir in remaining ½ cup milk before refrigerating.

4. Make sauce: In food processor, puree raspberries with syrup until smooth. Strain through sieve into bowl to remove seeds. Spoon sauce onto 8 dessert plates. Divide pudding among dishes.

NUTRIENT VALUE PER SERVING OF MY RICE PUDDING

245 calories, 5 g protein, 2 g fat (8% fat; 2 g saturated fat), 51 g carbohydrate, 123 mg sodium, 4 mg cholesterol

HEAVY CREAM RICE PUDDING

453 calories (almost twice the calories), 5 g fat (more than twice the fat)

TOASTY COCONUT

I'm sure you've all toasted marshmallows. Don't lie! Well, I love toasted coconut sprinkled over this pudding—I said sprinkled, not heaped. Remember, coconut does contain fat. Spread the coconut out in a thin, even layer on a baking sheet. Place in 325° oven until golden brown and smelling coconutty, about 10 minutes. Stir frequently. Here's an important tip: Watch carefully, because at the end it can scorch.

a palette of sauces

Clockwise from left: **APRICOT:** Puree canned, drained apricots, and sweeten to taste with a little sugar. **KIWIFRUIT:** Puree kiwifruit with a little drained, canned pear, and sweeten slightly. **STRAWBERRY:** Puree thawed, frozen strawberries in syrup. **PEACH:** Puree canned, drained peaches. **BLUEBERRY-STRAWBERRY:** Puree together thawed, frozen blueberries and thawed, frozen strawberries in syrup. **PEAR:** Puree canned, drained pears.

Zebra Parfaits

MAKES 2 SERVINGS EACH OF CHOCOLATE AND VANILLA PUDDINGS,
OR 4 PARFAITS

PREP: 10 MINUTES, PLUS CHILLING FOR
   EACH FLAVOR PUDDING

COOK: 6 MINUTES FOR EACH FLAVOR
   PUDDING

CHILL: 2 HOURS

PARFAIT ASSEMBLY: 15 MINUTES

Stripes are here to stay. Mother Nature dresses her zebras and tigers in them. The Kleins—Anne and Calvin—use them in their sportswear. And now, I've created striped food—my Zebra Parfait with its layers of creamy chocolate and vanilla puddings.

CHOCOLATE PUDDING

3 *tablespoons granulated sugar*

2 *tablespoons unsweetened cocoa powder*

2 *tablespoons boiling water*

2½ *tablespoons cornstarch*

1 *can (12 ounces) evaporated skim milk*

2 *teaspoons pure vanilla extract*

VANILLA PUDDING

2½ *tablespoons cornstarch*

1 *can (12 ounces) evaporated skim milk*

3 *tablespoons granulated sugar*

2 *teaspoons pure vanilla extract*

PARFAITS

1 *recipe Chocolate Pudding*

1 *recipe Vanilla Pudding*

2 *tablespoons chopped nuts, such as walnuts*
  or almonds

1 Make chocolate pudding: In small bowl, combine sugar and cocoa powder. Add 2 tablespoons boiling water and stir until smooth and shiny.

2 In second small bowl, stir together cornstarch and ¼ cup evaporated milk to dissolve cornstarch.

3 In medium saucepan, stir together remaining evaporated milk, cocoa mixture, and cornstarch mixture. Over medium-low heat, stir pudding continuously, until it thickens and comes to a boil, about 6 minutes. Stir in vanilla. Pour into serving bowl(s). Cool slightly. Press plastic wrap directly on surface. Refrigerate until thoroughly chilled, about 2 hours.

4 Make vanilla pudding: In bowl, stir cornstarch and ¼ cup evaporated milk to dissolve cornstarch.

5 In medium saucepan, stir remaining evaporated milk, sugar, and cornstarch mixture. Over medium-low heat, stir pudding continuously, until it thickens and comes to a boil, about 6 minutes. Stir in vanilla. Pour into serving bowl(s). Cool slightly. Press plastic wrap directly on surface. Refrigerate until thoroughly chilled, about 2 hours.

6 Assemble parfaits: For each of the 4 parfaits, in small, tall, parfait glass or dessert glass, layer the following: 2 tablespoons chocolate pudding, 2 tablespoons vanilla pudding, ½ teaspoon chopped nuts, and then repeat the layering twice more with the chocolate, vanilla, and nuts.

MARSHMALLOW VARIATION

For each pudding or parfait, count out 12 mini-marshmallows and cut each one in half with wet scissors. Toss into each serving of pudding, or use instead of vanilla pudding when layering the parfait, and/or use as a garnish.

NUTRIENT VALUE PER SERVING OF

MY CHOCOLATE PUDDING

283 calories, 14 g protein, 1 g fat (4% fat; 1 g saturated fat), 51 g carbohydrate, 196 mg sodium, 6 mg cholesterol

TRADITIONAL CHOCOLATE PUDDING

441 calories (more than 1½ times the calories), 20 g fat (20 times the fat)

NUTRIENT VALUE PER SERVING OF

MY VANILLA PUDDING

252 calories, 13 g protein, 0 g fat (0% fat; 0 g saturated fat), 48 g carbohydrate, 197 mg sodium, 6 mg cholesterol

TRADITIONAL VANILLA PUDDING

318 calories (1¼ times the calories), 12 g fat (compared to 0 fat)

NUTRIENT VALUE PER SERVING OF

MY ZEBRA PARFAIT

292 calories, 14 g protein, 3 g fat (10% fat; 1 g saturated fat), 50 g carbohydrate, 198 mg sodium, 6 mg cholesterol

TRADITIONAL PARFAIT

404 calories (1⅓ times the calories), 19 g fat (6⅓ times the fat)

Some-Like-It-Hot Chocolate Soufflés

MAKES 6 INDIVIDUAL SOUFFLÉS, OR ONE 6-SERVING SOUFFLÉ

PREP: 30 MINUTES

BAKE: AT 350° FOR 20 TO 25 MINUTES

Oh, don't be afraid to make a soufflé. People just hear the word soufflé and they begin to twitch. They think they need a white chef's jacket with their name embroidered over the pocket. And then, when the soufflé is actually in the oven, no one can breathe. Both the phone and the refrigerator have to be unplugged. Well, don't believe any of it. My individual soufflés make things real easy, since there is much less danger of collapse. So go ahead—plug the telephone and refrigerator back in, and get out your whisk.

Nonstick vegetable-oil cooking spray
Granulated sugar, for coating dishes
1 cup granulated sugar
⅓ cup unsweetened cocoa powder
2 tablespoons all-purpose flour
¾ teaspoon instant espresso coffee powder
¼ teaspoon salt
1 cup evaporated low-fat milk
½ ounce unsweetened chocolate, grated
3 tablespoons crème de cacao or coffee liqueur
2 teaspoons pure vanilla extract
5 large egg whites
¼ teaspoon cream of tartar
Confectioners' sugar, for dusting

1 Preheat oven to 350°. Coat six 10-ounce soufflé dishes (or one 2-quart soufflé dish) with nonstick cooking spray. Sprinkle with granulated sugar to coat and then tap out excess.

2 In medium saucepan, whisk together ¾ cup granulated sugar, cocoa powder, flour, espresso powder, and salt, until blended. Whisk in evaporated milk and unsweetened chocolate. Bring to a simmer over medium heat, whisking constantly. Cook, whisking, until thickened and chocolate is melted, 1 to 2 minutes. Remove from heat. Press waxed paper directly on surface. Let cool until just warm to the touch, 15 minutes. Whisk in crème de cacao and vanilla until blended.

3 In large bowl, with electric mixer on medium-high speed, beat together egg whites and cream of tartar until soft peaks form. Gradually beat in remaining ¼ cup granulated sugar, 1 tablespoon at a time, until stiff and glossy peaks form. Whisk one-quarter of egg whites into chocolate mixture to lighten. Fold remaining whites into chocolate mixture just until combined. Scrape into prepared dish(es).

4 Bake individual soufflés in 350° oven until puffed, and knife inserted near centers comes out clean, 20 to 25 minutes (or 35 to 40 minutes for 2-quart soufflé dish). Sift confectioners' sugar over top(s) and serve immediately.

NUTRIENT VALUE PER MY INDIVIDUAL SOUFFLÉ

221 calories, 8 g protein, 2 g fat (8% fat; 1 g saturated fat), 45 g carbohydrate, 185 mg sodium, 2 mg cholesterol

TRADITIONAL CHOCOLATE SOUFFLÉ

263 calories (1⅕ times the calories), 18 g fat (9 times the fat)

**NUTRIENT VALUE
PER MY ÉCLAIR**
177 calories, 5 g protein, 7 g fat
(35% fat; 2 g saturated fat),
24 g carbohydrate, 166 mg
sodium, 82 mg cholesterol
TRADITIONAL ÉCLAIR
347 calories (almost twice
the calories), 26 g fat (3¾ times
the fat)

Éclairs à l'Orange

MAKES 8 ÉCLAIRS

PREP: 35 MINUTES, PLUS CHILLING

BAKE: AT 375° FOR 35 TO 45 MINUTES

COOK: ABOUT 10 MINUTES

Okay—get out your pad and pencil, because now we're going to have a French lesson. The word *éclair*, in French, means "lightning" or "flash" —I always knew these pastries came from above. So what does this have to do with anything? Point a flashlight at the shiny glaze. Oooh, put your sunglasses on—see what I mean? It's like flashes of chocolate gold.

How did I create this recipe? Well, one morning I opened my refrigerator and there it was—half an éclair left over from the night before, just sitting there, staring at me. Now don't tell me you've never had leftover dessert for breakfast. I poured myself a glass of orange juice, took the éclair, and sat down at the kitchen table. The phone rang. I reached for it, knocking the juice over and splashing the éclair. Not being one to waste anything, I took a bite. It was sensational! Another recipe was born.

ÉCLAIRS

¾ cup water

3 tablespoons 70% buttermilk-vegetable oil spread

¼ teaspoon salt

¾ cup all-purpose flour

2 large whole eggs

1 large egg white

Nonstick vegetable-oil cooking spray

PASTRY CREAM

⅔ cup low-fat milk (1%)

3 tablespoons granulated sugar

4 teaspoons all-purpose flour

2 teaspoons cornstarch

Pinch salt

1 large egg yolk

1 teaspoon 70% buttermilk-vegetable oil spread

2 teaspoons grated orange zest

1 teaspoon orange extract

½ teaspoon pure vanilla extract

½ cup frozen nonfat nondairy whipped topping, thawed

CHOCOLATE GLAZE

¼ cup low-fat sweetened condensed milk

2 tablespoons unsweetened cocoa powder

2 to 4 teaspoons water, as needed

1. Make éclairs: In small, heavy saucepan, combine ¾ cup water, vegetable oil spread, and salt. Bring to a boil. When vegetable oil spread melts, remove from heat. Add flour all at once and mix rapidly with wooden spoon until mixture comes together in a ball. Place saucepan over low heat for 3 to 4 minutes to dry dough, mixing continually with wooden spoon. Dough should be soft and not stick to your fingers. Transfer dough to food processor or large bowl of a heavy-duty electric mixer. Cool 5 minutes.

2. Add whole eggs and egg white, one at a time, mixing until completely smooth after each addition. (This can be done by hand, but it is much easier in food processor or heavy-duty electric mixer.)

3. Coat baking sheet with nonstick cooking spray. Fill large pastry bag (without tip) with dough. Onto baking sheet, squeeze out 8 éclairs, each about 1 inch in

continued

diameter and about 4 inches in length. Let stand at least 30 minutes to dry.

4 Preheat oven to 375°.

5 Bake éclairs in 375° oven until golden and cooked all the way through, 35 to 45 minutes. Transfer to wire rack to cool.

6 *Meanwhile, make pastry cream:* In small, heavy saucepan, stir milk, sugar, flour, cornstarch, and salt, until blended. Cook over medium heat, stirring constantly, until mixture comes to a boil and thickens, 4 to 5 minutes. Remove from heat. In small bowl, lightly beat egg yolk. Gradually whisk in about ¼ cup hot milk mixture. Whisk egg yolk mixture back into milk mixture in pan. Return pan to medium-low heat and whisk mixture until it just barely begins to simmer, about 30 seconds. Remove from heat. Stir

in vegetable oil spread, orange zest, and orange and vanilla extracts, until smooth and melted. Transfer to bowl. Press plastic wrap directly onto surface. Cool to room temperature. Then chill thoroughly in refrigerator, about 2 hours. Fold in whipped topping. Refrigerate until ready to assemble.

7 *To assemble éclairs:* Cut each éclair in half lengthwise. Spoon about 2 tablespoons pastry cream into each éclair bottom. Replace tops.

8 *Make glaze:* In small saucepan, combine condensed milk and cocoa powder. Heat over low heat, stirring constantly, until mixture bubbles and thickens, 1 to 2 minutes. Spread over tops of éclairs. If glaze is too thick to spread, thin with 2 to 4 teaspoons of water. These are best eaten immediately or soon after making, and definitely the same day. (Make sure you invite friends over so you don't eat more than one!)

A Clafouti for All Seasons

MAKES 8 SERVINGS

PREP: 20 MINUTES

BAKE: AT 350° FOR 40 TO 50 MINUTES

I actually played a clafouti in the high school band— I was a clafloutist. No, wait a second—I'm confused. I was a flutist. A clafouti is a crustless custard tart—say that ten times with a piece of clafouti in your mouth. The French word *clafoutis* comes from the word *clafir*, meaning "to fill"—the custard batter flows around the fruit to fill up the baking dish.

I make this with fresh nectarines, plums, or apricots, but you can make it with any fruit in season—pears, apples, peaches, or cherries. But remember, you're to eat this, not play it.

Nonstick vegetable-oil cooking spray
8 ripe small nectarines, or plums or apricots,
   halved and pitted
2 large eggs
½ cup low-fat milk (1%)
½ cup + 1 tablespoon granulated sugar

¼ cup reduced-fat sour cream

3 tablespoons all-purpose flour

½ teaspoon pure vanilla extract

¼ teaspoon almond extract

Pinch salt

1 tablespoon sliced blanched almonds

1 Preheat oven to 350°. Coat 10-inch glass pie plate or 9 × 9 × 2-inch square baking dish with nonstick cooking spray.

2 In prepared pie plate, arrange nectarines, plums, or apricots, cut sides up, in single layer.

3 In large bowl, with electric mixer on medium speed, beat eggs until frothy. Add milk, ½ cup sugar, sour cream, flour, vanilla and almond extracts, and salt. Beat until very well blended, about 2 minutes. Pour batter over and around fruit in pie plate. Sprinkle top with remaining 1 tablespoon sugar. Sprinkle almonds over top.

4 Bake in 350° oven until puffed and lightly browned, 40 to 50 minutes. Serve warm or at room temperature. Cut into wedges.

NUTRIENT VALUE PER SERVING OF MY CLAFOUTI

142 calories, 4 g protein, 3 g fat (18% fat; 1 g saturated fat), 26 g carbohydrate, 45 mg sodium, 56 mg cholesterol

TRADITIONAL CLAFOUTI

330 calories (2⅓ times the fat), 21 g fat (7 times the fat)

The Royal Trifle

MAKES 10 SERVINGS

PREP: 40 MINUTES, PLUS CHILLING

COOK: 5 MINUTES

BAKE: CAKE ROLL AT 375° FOR
12 MINUTES

There I was, in Buckingham Palace. No, I hadn't
been invited for tea. I was with a small group touring
the palace. So much bric-a-brac. As we turned a corner, I could smell something baking. I sneaked off,
following the smell, and wound up in—you guessed
it—the royal kitchen. There was the Queen Mum,
dressed in an apron with her sleeves rolled up, and
tiaraless—it was such a shock to see her. It must
have been the cook's day off. She was slicing a jelly
roll, with a huge bowl of custard on the counter. I
bowed, and asked what she was making. "The Royal
Trifle, of course." Would you believe, we swapped
recipes—her trifle for my Pineapple Dream Boat
(page 170).

CUSTARD

¼ cup granulated sugar

2 tablespoons cornstarch

2 tablespoons all-purpose flour

⅛ teaspoon salt

1 large egg

3 cups low-fat milk (1%)

1 tablespoon 70% buttermilk-vegetable oil spread

2 teaspoons pure vanilla extract

SPONGE CAKE

Nonstick vegetable-oil cooking spray

⅔ cup cake flour

1 teaspoon baking powder

¼ teaspoon salt

2 large eggs

½ cup granulated sugar

3 tablespoons water

½ teaspoon pure vanilla extract

¼ teaspoon almond extract

Confectioners' sugar, for dusting

½ cup cherry jam

½ pint fresh strawberries, hulled

1 cup frozen pitted sweet cherries, thawed, drained,
and halved

1 kiwifruit, peeled, halved lengthwise, and sliced
crosswise

2 tablespoons sliced blanched almonds, toasted
(see To Toast or Not to Toast, page 31)

Frozen nonfat nondairy whipped topping, thawed
(optional)

1 *Make custard:* In medium bowl, whisk together
sugar, cornstarch, flour, and salt, until blended.
Whisk in egg and ½ cup milk, until blended. In
small saucepan, heat remaining 2½ cups milk over
medium heat until small bubbles appear around
edge of pan. Gradually whisk hot milk into egg mixture. Return to saucepan; cook over medium heat,
stirring constantly, until mixture thickens and comes
to a simmer, about 2 minutes. Reduce heat to low
and simmer, stirring, for 2 minutes longer. Remove
from heat. Stir in vegetable oil spread and vanilla,
until smooth. Pour into medium bowl. Press plastic
wrap directly onto surface and cool to room temperature. Refrigerate until cold, about 3 hours.

NUTRIENT VALUE PER SERVING OF MY TRIFLE

230 calories, 6 g protein, 4 g fat (17% fat; 2 g saturated fat), 42 g carbohydrate, 179 mg sodium, 70 mg cholesterol

THE CLASSIC TRIFLE

406 calories (1¾ times the calories), 14 g fat (3½ times the fat)

2 *Meanwhile, make cake:* Preheat oven to 375°. Line bottom of 13 × 9 × 2-inch baking pan with waxed paper. Lightly coat paper with cooking spray.

3 Into bowl, sift flour, baking powder, and salt.

4 In large bowl, with electric mixer on high speed, beat eggs until thick and pale yellow, about 5 minutes. Then gradually beat in granulated sugar. Add 3 tablespoons water and the vanilla and almond extracts. Reduce mixer speed to low, and beat until blended. Sift in flour mixture in three additions, and beat on low speed until just blended. Pour into prepared pan, gently spreading evenly.

5 Bake in 375° oven until top is golden, cake is springy to the touch, and a wooden pick inserted in center comes out clean, about 12 minutes. Cool cake in pan on wire rack for 5 minutes. Dust clean kitchen towel with confectioners' sugar. Turn cake out onto towel. Carefully peel off waxed paper. From long side, roll up cake and towel together. Let cool completely on rack.

6 *To assemble trifle:* Unroll cake and towel. Spread cake with jam. From same long side, roll up cake, without towel. With serrated knife, cut cake crosswise into ½-inch-thick slices. Arrange a few slices in

continued

bottom of 2-quart straight-sided glass bowl. Spread 1 cup chilled custard over top. Set aside 4 small strawberries for garnish. Slice remaining berries. Top custard in bowl with half the sliced berries and half the cherries. Arrange some cake slices around side of bowl so cut sides show through. Top fruit layer with remaining cake slices. Top with remaining strawberries and cherries. Top with remaining custard, spreading to cover fruit. Cover with plastic wrap and refrigerate at least 4 hours, or overnight.

7 To serve, cut reserved strawberries in half. Garnish top of trifle with kiwifruit slices, strawberry halves, toasted almonds, and whipped topping, if using.

don't let your cake roll

Not only do you get the Royal Trifle in this recipe, you also get the Royal Roll. Be sure to roll up your cake and the towel together to cool—this prevents the cake from cracking. If you'd like, you can skip the trifle, and serve just the roll, dusted with a little confectioners' sugar.

Bread Pudding with a Flair

MAKES 8 SERVINGS

PREP: 15 MINUTES

COOK: ABOUT 5 MINUTES

BAKE: BREAD AT 350° FOR 7 MINUTES;
BREAD PUDDING AT 350° FOR 35
MINUTES

Just put a bowl of pudding, custard, or anything creamy in front of me, and you'll witness something unusual—me not talking. I had an aunt who made the best bread pudding. It had a special sweetness— but she would never tell us her secret. One afternoon after I had just finished a bowl of her pudding, and when no one was looking, I went into the kitchen and peeked in her garbage basket. Please

don't think any less of me, but that's what I did. I lifted up the tea bags, and there was the telltale evidence, sitting right on top—pear cores! So the pear was the flair.

Nonstick vegetable-oil cooking spray
4 ounces Italian or French bread, sliced ½ inch thick
2 tablespoons fresh lemon juice
1 tablespoon + ½ cup packed light-brown sugar
1 teaspoon butter
1 pound ripe pears, such as Bartlett, peeled, quartered, cored, and thinly sliced lengthwise (2¼ cups)
3 tablespoons all-purpose flour
2½ cups low-fat milk (1%)
⅓ cup reduced-fat sour cream

1 large whole egg
2 large egg whites
½ teaspoon pure vanilla extract
¼ teaspoon salt

TOPPING

1 teaspoon butter
2 teaspoons light-brown sugar

1 Place oven rack in upper third of oven. Preheat oven to 350°. Lightly coat 9 × 9 × 2-inch square glass baking dish with nonstick cooking spray. Set aside. Place bread slices on baking sheet. Toast in upper third of 350° oven until lightly crisped and golden brown, about 7 minutes. Set slices aside. Leave oven on.

2 In large skillet over medium heat, stir together lemon juice, 1 tablespoon brown sugar, and butter, until mixture has melted and is bubbly, about 1 minute. Add pears and cook, tossing frequently, until tender, about 4 minutes. (Timing may vary, depending upon ripeness of pears.)

3 Layer bread and pear mixture in prepared dish.

4 In medium bowl, whisk together remaining ½ cup brown sugar and the flour. Whisk in milk, sour cream, whole egg, egg whites, vanilla, and salt. Pour over bread and fruit. *For topping:* Dot top with butter and sprinkle with brown sugar.

5 Bake, uncovered, in upper third of 350° oven until just set, about 35 minutes. Serve warm.

NUTRIENT VALUE PER SERVING OF MY BREAD PUDDING

193 calories, 7 g protein, 4 g fat (18% fat; 2 g saturated fat), 34 g carbohydrate, 224 mg sodium, 36 mg cholesterol

TRADITIONAL BREAD PUDDING

367 calories (almost twice the calories), 22 g fat (5½ times the fat)

Josephine's Napoleon

MAKES 10 NAPOLEONS

PREP: 30 MINUTES, PLUS CHILLING

BAKE: PASTRY AT 375° FOR 8 MINUTES

COOK: 5 TO 7 MINUTES

We all know Napoleon had a problem with height. People were always making short jokes, and Josephine just felt awful about it. So, she decided to give his ego a boost. She created a very tall dessert for him, and called it—you guessed it—Napoleon. It was layers and layers of pastry and filling—in fact, it was taller than he was. It was so tall, she could barely get it to the table without it falling over. Since I have no problem with height, even though I'm only five-six without my aerobics shoes on, I've made a much shorter version.

Nonstick vegetable-oil cooking spray

PASTRY

7 sheets (17 × 12 inches) frozen phyllo dough, thawed according to package directions

1½ tablespoons canola oil

1 tablespoon butter, melted

7½ teaspoons granulated sugar

PASTRY CREAM

½ cup granulated sugar

2 tablespoons all-purpose flour

1 tablespoon cornstarch

Pinch salt

1¾ cups low-fat milk (1%)

1 large egg

¼ teaspoon almond extract

¼ teaspoon pure vanilla extract

1 tablespoon butter

1 can (11 ounces) mandarin oranges, drained

1 cup diced (½-inch pieces) drained canned pineapple (juice packed)

2 tablespoons confectioners' sugar, for dusting

1. Preheat oven to 375°. Lightly coat large sideless baking sheet with nonstick cooking spray (you may use an inverted jelly-roll pan, if you'd like). Place phyllo on clean, dry surface. Cover lightly with waxed paper and then with a slightly dampened towel, to prevent drying out.

2. *Make pastry:* Place sheet of waxed paper on work surface. In small dish, stir together oil and butter. Lift 1 sheet of phyllo onto waxed paper. Keep remaining sheets covered. Brush lightly with butter-oil mixture and sprinkle evenly with 1¼ teaspoons of the sugar. Repeat with remaining sheets of phyllo, stacking one on top of the other. Do not sprinkle top layer with sugar.

3. Place entire stack of phyllo on prepared baking sheet. Using sharp knife or pizza wheel cutter, cut stack in thirds lengthwise. Cut each third crosswise into ten 1¾-inch-wide strips, to make a total of 30 rectangles. (If you want phyllo rectangles to be less puffy and flatter after baking, lightly coat bottom of another large baking sheet or 2 smaller sheets with nonstick cooking spray. Place baking sheet[s], coated side down, directly on top of phyllo.)

4. Bake phyllo in 375° oven until just puffy (if not covered) and beginning to color, about 8 minutes. (If covered with baking sheet, remove sheet after 8 minutes and return phyllo to oven. Bake until tops

NUTRIENT VALUE PER MY NAPOLEON
173 calories, 3 g protein, 6 g fat (31% fat; 2 g saturated fat), 27 g carbohydrate, 107 mg sodium, 29 mg cholesterol

TRADITIONAL NAPOLEON
335 calories (almost twice the calories), 17 g fat (almost 3 times the fat)

are golden brown and crisp, another 1 to 2 minutes.) With metal spatula, immediately loosen rectangles from baking sheets and transfer to wire racks to cool.

5 *Make pastry cream:* In small saucepan, stir together sugar, flour, cornstarch, and salt, until blended. Whisk in milk. Place over medium heat and cook, stirring, until mixture comes to a boil and thickens, 4 to 6 minutes. In small bowl, beat egg. Whisk in about ½ cup hot milk mixture. Stir egg mixture into milk mixture in saucepan. Return pan to medium-low heat, and stir constantly, just until it begins to simmer, about 1 minute. Remove from heat. Stir in

almond and vanilla extracts and butter, until melted. Press waxed paper directly on surface. Let cool.

6 Place oranges and pineapple on paper towels to drain well. Reserve 6 orange segments for garnish.

7 Spoon pastry cream into plastic food-storage bag and snip off ½ inch of corner. Pipe 2 lines of pastry cream down center of 10 phyllo rectangles. Arrange half the fruit on top of pastry cream. Top with 10 more phyllo rectangles. Repeat with cream and fruit, and top with remaining 10 rectangles. With fine-mesh sieve, dust tops with confectioners' sugar.

Oh what temptations these juicy fruits bring,
Apples and pears and peaches that cling!

Nature's desserts in their prettiest dresses,
Garnished to perfectly show off their tresses.

Release your resistance, relax and give in—
The dishes I've made only taste full of sin!

With fruit that is naturally sweet, ripe, and tender,
This "Garden of Eden" emerges in splendor!

In the Garden of Eden

Cozy Cobbler

MAKES 10 SERVINGS

*I*f I'm feeling *verklemmt* (choked up or overcome with emotion), which happens more than you might think, I find a cozy cobbler comforts me. The luscious fruit mixture with all its rich juices soaks into the buttermilk biscuit topping. Have you noticed that the biscuits look like cobblestones? That's how the cobbler got its name.

Now, let me tell you a secret. I've added a sprinkling of black pepper to the filling—not enough to make you sneeze, but just enough to tickle your tongue.

FILLING

½ cup granulated sugar

2 teaspoons cornstarch

⅛ teaspoon ground black pepper

2½ cups frozen peach slices, unthawed

1½ cups frozen dry-pack blueberries, unthawed

1 tablespoon fresh lemon juice

BISCUIT TOPPING

1 cup all-purpose flour

5 tablespoons granulated sugar

1 teaspoon baking powder

½ teaspoon baking soda

¼ teaspoon salt

3 tablespoons 70% buttermilk-vegetable oil spread, cut into pieces and chilled

1 large egg

3 tablespoons low-fat buttermilk

1. Preheat oven to 375°.

2. *Make filling:* In medium saucepan, stir sugar, cornstarch, and pepper, until combined. Stir in peach slices, blueberries, and lemon juice and let stand.

3. *Meanwhile, make biscuit topping:* In medium bowl, stir together flour, sugar, baking powder, baking soda, and salt. With pastry blender, 2 knives held like scissors, or your fingertips, cut in vegetable oil spread until mixture resembles coarse meal. In small bowl, stir together egg and buttermilk. Make well in center of flour mixture, add egg mixture, and stir until just combined. Transfer to lightly floured work surface and pat out to rectangle ½ inch thick. With small heart-shaped or other shaped cookie cutter, cut out shapes. Reroll scraps and cut out more shapes (you should have 10 shapes total).

4. Stir cornstarch-fruit mixture over medium heat. Bring to a boil, stirring gently. Pour into 9-inch pie plate. Place biscuits on top.

5. Bake in 375° oven until biscuits are golden brown and filling is bubbly, about 25 minutes. If biscuits begin to brown too quickly, loosely cover with aluminum foil for last 15 minutes of baking. Serve warm or at room temperature.

NUTRIENT VALUE PER SERVING OF MY COBBLER

177 calories, 3 g protein, 4 g fat (19% fat; 1 g saturated fat), 34 g carbohydrate, 195 mg sodium, 21 mg cholesterol

TRADITIONAL COBBLER

272 calories (more than 1½ times the calories), 10 g fat (2½ times the fat)

so what do cranes have to do with it?

Get ready for a history lesson. I've talked before in this book about cranberries, but I didn't tell you where the name came from. Now I will. They were first called bounceberries, because when they're ripe, they bounce all around. But that sounded funny—not like something you would want to eat. Then people noticed there were cranes walking through the bogs, snacking on the crimson berries. That's it—we'll call them craneberries. But after a while, "crane" became "cran"—you know how people in New England talk. So, the third name was the one that stuck. By the way, have you ever eaten a raw cranberry? I did, and my lips wouldn't unpucker for a week!

Apple-Cranberry Crumble

MAKES 10 SERVINGS

PREP: 15 MINUTES

BAKE: AT 375° FOR 40 TO 45 MINUTES

Crumble? This could make a great Steven Spielberg movie. The opening shot is in the kitchen. It's dawn. Sunlight is just beginning to filter through the curtains. The camera pans in on a table. Sitting there are an empty cereal bowl and an opened box of oat cereal. The house begins to shake, the camera moves back, the box tips over, spilling oats everywhere, and the walls begin to crumble, and . . . No, stop! Wrong movie. This is really a dessert invented by the English, with a crunchy topping like crumbled cookies. Let's start over. Long shot of English country house. Close-up: Butler comes into drawing room carrying silver tray with elegant serving dish and says, "Madame, your crumble is served."

Nonstick vegetable-oil cooking spray

FILLING

4 to 5 *Golden Delicious apples, peeled, quartered, cored, and thinly sliced (8 cups)*

1½ *cups fresh or frozen cranberries*

⅓ *cup packed light-brown sugar*

2 *tablespoons all-purpose flour*

1 *teaspoon ground cinnamon*

CRUMBLE TOPPING

½ *cup old-fashioned rolled oats*

6 *tablespoons all-purpose flour*

¼ *cup packed light-brown sugar*

¼ *teaspoon baking powder*

¼ *teaspoon salt*

1½ *tablespoons vegetable oil*

1 *tablespoon fruit juice, preferably apple or cranberry*

1 *container (8 ounces) nonfat plain or vanilla yogurt (optional)*

1 Preheat oven to 375°. Lightly coat 9 × 9 × 2-inch square baking pan with nonstick cooking spray.

2 *Make filling:* In large bowl, toss together apples, cranberries, brown sugar, flour, and cinnamon. Transfer to prepared baking pan.

3 *Make topping:* In medium bowl, stir together oats, flour, brown sugar, baking powder, and salt, until no lumps of brown sugar remain. In small bowl, stir together oil and fruit juice. Drizzle juice mixture over oat mixture and toss until evenly moistened and crumbly. Press together small handfuls of oat mixture to make streusel-like pieces, and arrange on top of apple filling to cover.

4 Bake in 375° oven until topping is browned and filling is bubbly, 40 to 45 minutes. Transfer pan to wire rack to cool slightly. Serve warm with a dollop of yogurt, if desired.

NUTRIENT VALUE PER SERVING OF MY CRUMBLE

146 calories, 2 g protein, 3 g fat (16% fat; 0 g saturated fat), 31 g carbohydrate, 67 mg sodium, 0 mg cholesterol

TRADITIONAL CRUMBLE

268 calories (almost twice the calories), 12 g fat (4 times the fat)

WHAT? CRANBERRIES OUT OF SEASON!

If fresh or frozen cranberries are on vacation, dried cranberries plumped in a little warm water will do the trick.

Dippity-Doo-Da Fondue with Fruit

MAKES 48 PIECES OF FRUIT, DIPPED

PREP: 15 MINUTES

COOK: 5 MINUTES

You've heard of the Big Dipper? The Little Dipper? I'm a huge dipper—I love to dip everything. In fact, everybody on the planet loves to dip. Italians dip their bread in olive oil, Mexicans dip their tortilla chips in salsa, and Syrians dip their pita bread in hummus. And we all remember the fondue craze, when nothing was safe. People were grabbing pork chops, chicken wings, and even French fries, and dipping them into everything from cheese to chocolate. I bet you didn't know there is actually a Universal Dipping Association where you can take classes in the proper technique of dipping and fonduing—not to be confused with skipping and canoeing.

½ ounce unsweetened chocolate, chopped

1 can (12 ounces) fat-free sweetened condensed milk

½ teaspoon pure vanilla extract

¼ cup unsweetened cocoa powder

48 assorted fruit dippers (large strawberries, banana slices, orange segments, apple slices, and/or fat-free poundcake cubes)

1 In small saucepan, combine unsweetened chocolate and 3 tablespoons condensed milk. Heat over medium-low heat, stirring constantly, until chocolate is melted. Stir in remaining condensed milk and the vanilla. Remove pan from heat. Sift cocoa powder on top, and then stir in until blended.

2 Return saucepan to medium-low heat and cook, stirring constantly, until mixture just begins to simmer. Remove from heat, and pour into a serving bowl or glass. On a decorative plate, arrange strawberries, other fruit, and poundcake cubes for dipping.

TOO COOL

When the chocolate sauce cools, it will thicken. So, you may need to reheat it and thin it a bit. Reheat over low heat, or in microwave in a small bowl at 100% power for 20 seconds, thinning with low-fat milk for desired dipping consistency.

NUTRIENT VALUE PER STRAWBERRY DIPPED IN MY CHOCOLATE

37 calories, 1 g protein, 0 g fat (0% fat; 0 g saturated fat), 8 g carbohydrate, 8 mg sodium, 0 mg cholesterol

NUTRIENT VALUE PER TABLESPOON OF SAUCE

34 calories, 1 g protein, 0 g fat (0% fat; 0 g saturated fat), 7 g carbohydrate, 11 mg sodium, 0 mg cholesterol

THE CLASSIC CHOCOLATE DIPPING SAUCE

71 calories (twice the calories), 4 g fat (compared to 0 fat)

something melty

Fondue (pronounced fahn-DOO) comes from the French word *fondre*, which means to melt. And the word *foundry* is a distant cousin—you know, that place where they melt metal. Although it's nice to have long fondue forks to spear the fruit and then dip it with a sweeping flourish, wooden picks will do fine. You'll just have to be a little less theatrical.

Georgia Baked Stuffed Peaches

MAKES 4 SERVINGS

PREP: 20 MINUTES

BAKE: AT 400° FOR 25 TO 30 MINUTES

I'm sure you've heard of the Georgia peach. And you've probably had peaches with a Melba sauce, with heavy cream, in ice cream, and in pie. But have you ever had one stuffed with cookies and baked? Well I have, and now I'm sharing my recipe with you. The first one I ever tasted was in a little hilltop trattoria overlooking Siena . . . don't get me started!

Even though there is a liqueur in this dessert, all the alcohol cooks off during the baking, leaving just the almond flavor.

- 4 medium-size peaches (not too ripe; about 1¾ pounds)
- 4 teaspoons butter, at room temperature
- 1 teaspoon unsweetened cocoa powder
- ⅓ cup (about ½ ounce) gingersnap cookies, crumbled
- 2 tablespoons light-brown sugar
- ¼ cup Amaretto or almond-flavored liqueur (1 miniature bottle)
- ¼ cup water
- 4 tablespoons nonfat plain or vanilla yogurt or reduced-fat sour cream (optional)

1 Preheat oven to 400°.

2 Halve peaches and remove pits. Scoop out about 1 tablespoon of peach flesh from each half. Chop coarsely and set aside. Cut thin slice from bottom of each peach half so each sits steady. Place peaches in baking dish just large enough to fit 8 halves.

3 In small bowl, stir together butter and cocoa powder until smooth. Stir in crumbled gingersnaps and reserved chopped peach. Divide stuffing equally among peach halves. Sprinkle with brown sugar and drizzle liqueur over peaches. Into baking dish, pour ¼ cup water around peaches.

4 Bake in 400° oven until fruit is just tender when pierced with knife, 25 to 30 minutes. Place 2 halves on each dessert plate. Pour any juices remaining in baking dish over peaches. Serve hot or warm. Top each serving with 1 tablespoon nonfat yogurt or reduced-fat sour cream, if desired.

NUTRIENT VALUE PER SERVING OF MY PEACHES

117 calories, 1 g protein, 4 g fat (32% fat; 3 g saturated fat), 19 g carbohydrate, 26 mg sodium, 10 mg cholesterol

TRADITIONAL STUFFED PEACHES

210 calories (1¾ times the calories), 5 g fat (1¼ times the fat)

amaretti cookies

Instead of filling the peaches with crushed gingersnaps, you can use amaretti. These macaroon cookies are very crunchy. If you eat them on their own, make sure to chew with your mouth closed, or people will turn and stare. The wonderful flavor of the cookies is a perfect match with the peaches. Crushed vanilla wafers or chocolate wafers also make a delicious filling.

Martha's Cherry-Pear Cobblers

MAKES 6 INDIVIDUAL COBBLERS

PREP: 20 MINUTES, PLUS CHILLING

BAKE: AT 400° FOR 25 TO 30 MINUTES

We all know the story about George Washington cutting down the cherry tree. But why did he do it? What was he so angry about? Did he still harbor ill feelings toward the British? And did you know that he actually butchered an entire orchard, including pear trees? Martha heard all the racket, hiked up her skirts, and ran outside. There was George, surrounded by all this fruit on the ground. Being a good housewife who hated waste, Martha gathered up all the fruit, raced inside, and made cobblers for the whole family and the entire staff. And here's the recipe I've adapted from Martha's cookbook.

LATTICE-TOP CRUST

½ cup all-purpose flour

1 tablespoon granulated sugar

¼ teaspoon baking powder

2 tablespoons 70% buttermilk-vegetable oil spread, cut into small pieces and chilled

2 tablespoons nonfat sour cream

FILLING

1 bag (12 ounces) frozen dry-pack cherries

2 medium-size pears, peeled, quartered, cored, and cut into ½-inch dice

¼ cup granulated sugar

4 teaspoons cornstarch

½ teaspoon grated lemon zest

1 tablespoon fresh lemon juice

1. *Make lattice-top crust:* In medium bowl, stir together flour, sugar, and baking powder. With pastry blender, 2 knives held like scissors, or your fingertips, cut in vegetable oil spread until mixture resembles coarse meal. Stir in sour cream just until combined. Knead very lightly to combine. Shape into disk, wrap in plastic wrap, and refrigerate several hours or overnight.

2. Preheat oven to 400°.

3. Pat dough out into 8 × 2-inch rectangle. Between two sheets of waxed paper, roll dough out to 18 × 4-inch strip. Remove top sheet of waxed paper. Cut crosswise into twenty-four ¾-inch-wide strips. Set aside.

4. *Make filling:* In medium bowl, toss together cherries, pears, sugar, cornstarch, lemon zest, and lemon juice. Divide equally among six 6-ounce ramekins or custard cups, about 3¾ inches across top. Top each with 4 dough strips to make lattice-top crust. Place on foil-covered baking sheet.

5. Bake in 400° oven until crust is golden and filling is bubbly, 25 to 30 minutes. Serve warm.

NUTRIENT VALUE PER MY INDIVIDUAL COBBLER

204 calories, 2 g protein, 4 g fat (16% fat; 1 g saturated fat), 42 g carbohydrate, 52 mg sodium, 0 mg cholesterol

TRADITIONAL COBBLER

378 calories (more than 1¾ times the calories), 10 g fat (2½ times the fat)

Crepes à la Barbra

MAKES 8 SERVINGS

PREP: 30 MINUTES

COOK: 16 MINUTES

BAKE: AT 375° FOR 10 MINUTES

In 1964, I was sixteen and went to New York City to
see Barbra Streisand in *Funny Girl*, and to visit the
World's Fair (see World's Fair Waffles, page 164).
To make a long story short, I had one ticket to see a
matinee at the Winter Garden Theater, but wound
up seeing five shows and sleeping on the floor of the
lighting booth. Fred, one of the lighting technicians,
would run across the street to a deli and buy me
knishes and blintzes for dinner. Being from New
Orleans, I had no idea what these were. In his thick
Brooklyn accent, he explained that they were just
like the crepes I got in New Orleans—I thought he
was saying drapes! Finally I figured out what he
meant—these were Hebrew National crepes. Now
you understand why crepes are so important in my
life. And still to this day, whenever I walk past the
Winter Garden Theater in New York—you know
what's been playing there forever—I just start
singing, "People. People who love blintzes . . ."

CREPES

¾ cup low-fat milk (1%)

¾ cup all-purpose flour

1 large egg

1 tablespoon honey

1 tablespoon 70% buttermilk-vegetable oil spread,
  melted

½ teaspoon pure vanilla extract

⅛ teaspoon salt

Nonstick vegetable-oil cooking spray

TOPPING

1 can (about 16 ounces) apricot halves, in syrup

3 tablespoons apricot jam

1 tablespoon honey

1 teaspoon grated orange zest

FILLING

3 ounces cream cheese, at room temperature

¼ cup confectioners' sugar

1½ cups low-fat (1%) whipped cottage cheese or nonfat
  farmer cheese

2 teaspoons grated orange zest

1 teaspoon pure vanilla extract

1 *Make crepes:* In blender or food processor, combine
milk, flour, egg, honey, vegetable oil spread, vanilla,
and salt, and blend until smooth. Or, whisk in bowl.

2 Lightly coat 10-inch nonstick skillet with nonstick
cooking spray. Heat over medium heat. Off heat,
add 3 tablespoons batter, swirling pan to evenly
coat bottom. Return to heat and cook until lightly
browned on bottom, about 2 minutes. Place, cooked
side up, on waxed paper. Repeat with remaining batter, coating skillet with nonstick cooking spray as
needed, making total of 8 crepes. Stack crepes with
waxed paper in between. (Can be made up to 2 days
ahead; store in airtight container, refrigerated.)

3 *Make topping:* Drain apricots, reserving ¼ cup
syrup. Cut apricot halves in half, if you'd like. In
small skillet, combine reserved syrup, jam, honey,
and orange zest. Bring to simmer over medium heat.
Add apricots and return to simmer. Set aside.

**NUTRIENT VALUE
PER MY CREPE**
205 calories, 9 g protein, 6 g fat
(25% fat; 3 g saturated fat),
30 g carbohydrate, 272 mg
sodium, 14 mg cholesterol
TRADITIONAL CREPE
313 calories (1½ times the
calories), 13 g fat (6½ times
the fat)

4 *Make filling:* In small bowl, stir together cream cheese and confectioners' sugar, until smooth. Stir in cottage cheese, orange zest, and vanilla.

5 Preheat oven to 375°. Coat 13 × 9 × 2-inch baking dish with nonstick cooking spray. Lay out crepes, cooked side down. Spoon about ¼ cup of filling in center of each crepe. Fold one side over filling. Leaving opposite side open, fold other 2 sides over filling to overlap in center. Place in prepared baking dish.

6 Bake in 375° oven until heated through and slightly crisp, about 10 minutes. Gently rewarm apricot topping over medium-low heat.

7 To serve, place a crepe on each of 8 dessert plates. Top with warm apricot topping.

lollipop variations

CHERRY: Substitute ½ teaspoon cherry extract for orange extract, and red food coloring for orange.

STRAWBERRY: Substitute ½ teaspoon strawberry extract for orange extract, and red food coloring for orange.

LEMON: Substitute ½ teaspoon lemon extract for orange extract, and yellow food coloring for orange.

BLUE MINT: Substitute ½ teaspoon peppermint extract for orange extract, and 1 or 2 drops blue food coloring for orange.

COCONUT: Substitute ½ teaspoon coconut extract for orange extract, and omit any food coloring.

Hey, Sucker!

MAKES 12 LOLLIPOPS

PREP: 20 MINUTES.

COOK: ABOUT 15 MINUTES

Admit it. You've never had a homemade sucker. You've always bought them. Well, as I've traveled from state to state, I've always searched out sucker factories. I've talked to head sucker makers and gotten all their secret recipes for all kinds of flavors, which I include here in my recipe. However, there are some rules that come with suckers. Never bite a sucker. Never chew on a sucker. A sucker is meant to be licked. The whole secret, which I learned from a ninety-three-year-old lady sucker maker in Cleveland, is to keep licking until all that's left is the stick. Then you get to make a wish. But if you bite into it, it's over.

Nonstick vegetable-oil cooking spray
12 lollipop sticks (each 4 inches long)
½ cup granulated sugar
2 tablespoons water
2 tablespoons light corn syrup
½ teaspoon orange extract
Orange food coloring

1 Lightly coat large baking sheet or 18-inch length of aluminum foil with nonstick cooking spray. Arrange lollipop sticks evenly spaced on baking sheet or foil, at least 6 inches apart.

2 In heavy, 1-quart saucepan, bring sugar, 2 tablespoons water, and corn syrup to boiling over medium heat. Cover saucepan and boil 5 minutes so any sugar crystals on side of pan wash down. Uncover and attach candy thermometer to side of pan.

3 Continue to boil, uncovered, until mixture reaches 280°. Lower heat so candy mixture doesn't start to caramelize; you don't want mixture to turn golden, since that would affect final color of lollipops. When candy thermometer reaches 300°, remove pan from heat. Let stand until all bubbles have calmed down.

4 Gently stir in orange extract and enough food coloring so candy mixture is vibrant orange color. Stir as gently as possible, since too much stirring will cause mixture to solidify into hard, sugary lump.

5 Working quickly, because mixture will harden as it cools, and using metal tablespoon, carefully pour 1 tablespoon of candy mixture over end of each lollipop stick, covering about 1 inch of stick.

6 Let lollipops cool completely. Carefully slide each lollipop off baking sheet or foil. Blot side resting on baking sheet or foil with paper towel to remove any cooking spray. Wrap each lollipop individually in plastic wrap.

STUCK-ON GOO

The best way to clean hardened candy from the saucepan and thermometer is to fill saucepan with hot tap water, place thermometer in water, and bring water to a boil. Hardened candy will dissolve. Then wash saucepan and thermometer.

NUTRIENT VALUE PER MY LOLLIPOP

42 calories, 0 g protein, 0 g fat (0 % fat; 0 g saturated fat), 11 g carbohydrate, 4 mg sodium, 0 mg cholesterol

LOLLIPOPS ARE LOLLIPOPS ARE LOLLIPOPS

They all have about the same calories (if same size), and they're all fat-free.

World's Fair Waffles with Blackberry-Nectarine Sauce

MAKES 6 SERVINGS

PREP: 20 MINUTES

COOK: SAUCE FOR 6 MINUTES; WAFFLES
FOR 3 TO 4 MINUTES PER BATCH

We were all there, right? The 1964 World's Fair in Flushing Meadow, New York—that's where I discovered these waffles. The first thing I wanted to see was the *Pietà* by Michelangelo, so I walked over to its special pavilion. Well, the line was so long, I felt I needed a little something to take with me. Right there was a waffle stand—perfect. The guard at the entrance thought differently. He said, "Let me hold that for you." I should have suspected. I had read "Little Red Riding Hood." I walked into the darkened pavilion, and there was the statue, against a wall of twinkling lights. I was breathless—it was a vision. When I returned to the bright sunlight, I walked over to the guard and said, "Thank you. Where's my waffle?" He looked right through me, as if I weren't there. And then I noticed a little blue stain on his shirt! That's when I decided I had to learn how to make these waffles myself.

SAUCE

½ cup granulated sugar

½ cup water

2½ cups sliced nectarines

1½ cups blackberries, fresh or frozen dry-pack

WAFFLES

1 cup all-purpose flour

1 teaspoon baking powder

½ teaspoon baking soda

¼ teaspoon ground cinnamon

¼ teaspoon salt

¾ cup low-fat buttermilk

2 tablespoons 70% buttermilk-vegetable oil spread, melted

1 large egg yolk

1 tablespoon light-brown sugar

1 teaspoon pure vanilla extract

3 large egg whites

Nonstick butter-flavored cooking spray

1 pint nonfat vanilla frozen yogurt (optional)

1 nectarine, pitted and sliced, for garnish (optional)

1 *Make sauce:* In medium saucepan, stir together sugar and ½ cup water. Over medium heat, bring to a boil, stirring. Add nectarines and blackberries. Bring to a simmer and continue simmering until nectarines are fork-tender, about 6 minutes. Set aside.

2 *Make waffles:* Into medium bowl, sift together flour, baking powder, baking soda, cinnamon, and salt. In another medium bowl, whisk together buttermilk, vegetable oil spread, egg yolk, brown sugar, and vanilla. Stir flour mixture into buttermilk mixture and stir until smooth.

3 In clean medium bowl, with electric mixer on medium speed, beat egg whites until stiff and glossy peaks form. Fold whites into batter.

NUTRIENT VALUE
PER MY WAFFLE

255 calories, 6 g protein, 5 g fat
(18% fat; 1 g saturated fat),
47 g carbohydrate, 351 mg
sodium, 37 mg cholesterol

TRADITIONAL WAFFLE

370 calories (almost 1½ times the
calories), 17 g fat (more than
2 ¾ times the fat)

FROZEN FROM THE GARDEN

To make these all year, you can
use fresh or frozen peaches
instead of the nectarines.

4   Preheat oven to lowest setting and place a wire rack
on top of middle oven rack. Heat waffle iron according to manufacturer's directions. Lightly coat with
nonstick cooking spray. Add batter to iron, using
about ½ cup for each waffle. Close waffle iron and
cook until waffles are golden brown, 3 to 4 minutes.
Slide cooked waffles onto wire rack in oven to stay
warm while making remaining waffles. Do not cover

waffles, or they will get soggy. Repeat with remaining batter, coating waffle iron with nonstick cooking
spray each time, for a total of 6 waffles. Gently
reheat sauce.

5   To serve, divide into individual waffles. Place a waffle on each of 6 dessert plates. Top with scoop of
frozen yogurt, if you like, and the warm sauce. Garnish with nectarine slices, if desired.

Cutting Up with Mother Nature

MAKES 6 SERVINGS (2 LARGE PLATES FOR SERVING)

PREP: 30 MINUTES

When you go to a restaurant and order a fruit plate, or even a vegetable plate, it's embarrassing! You look at it and say, "What's this? Would you honestly serve this to Mother Nature if she were here?" Now, if Mother Nature were coming to my house for dinner, I would make this beautiful "flower," using the best of Mother's fruit from her own gardens. This is not hard to do. Just look for the ripest melons and pineapples and other fruit, get out your knife, and use your imagination. Make the flower in my picture, or go out in your garden, pick a lovely flower, and use that for a model. All right—I admit it. I have done a portrait of Cindy Crawford in papaya.

16 thin (¼ inch) quarter-circle slices watermelon, radius about 4 inches (without rind)

16 thin (¼ inch) half-circle slices fresh pineapple (without shell and core)

10 medium red grapes, sliced in thirds

16 thin (¼ inch) slices honeydew melon (without rind), leaf-shaped

Lime wedges and confectioners' sugar (optional)

1. Stack watermelon slices, 4 at a time, and round off both corners of the rounded side. Cut ∨-shape from rounded side, opposite point, to form heart shape. Arrange 8 pieces on serving plate, in a circle with diameter about 7 inches. Repeat with remaining melon on second serving plate. You can place any trimmings under rounded edges of slices to make them stand up slightly.

2. On each plate, arrange half the pineapple slices, slightly overlapping in loose circle, in center of plate where points of watermelon slices come together. On each plate, cluster grapes in center.

3. Stack honeydew slices, 4 at a time, and cut small ∨-shape wedges from sides. Cut thin sliver for "vein" from center of each "leaf ." Repeat with remaining melon. On each plate, arrange 8 leaves around outside, tucking under edges of watermelon hearts. Serve with lime wedges and dust lightly with confectioners' sugar, if desired.

NUTRIENT VALUE PER SERVING OF MY FRUIT PLATE

116 calories, 2 g protein, 1g fat (8% fat; 0 g saturated fat), 28 g carbohydrate, 13 mg sodium, 0 mg cholesterol

WHERE'S THE FAT?

Would you believe the fat is in the watermelon? Who would have thought?

Uptown Baked Apple

MAKES 4 SERVINGS

PREP: 30 MINUTES

BAKE: AT 375° FOR 30 TO 35 MINUTES

The everyday, ordinary baked apple goes into the oven looking very perky, and then comes out very sad—wrinkled and saggy. It's like that portrait of Dorian Gray. Not a nice fate for an apple. I treat my baked apple much more lovingly. I top it with the tiniest bit of butter—that's right, butter—and a little apricot jam. For the crowning touch, I wrap the whole thing in an elegant phyllo coat. Now it's ready for a special evening out.

Nonstick vegetable-oil cooking spray

4 small McIntosh apples (about 5 ounces each)

¾ cup diced mixed dried fruit

2 teaspoons butter

4 tablespoons apricot jam

8 sheets (17 × 12 inches) frozen phyllo dough, thawed according to package directions

2 tablespoons reduced-fat sour cream (optional)

Ground cinnamon, for garnish (optional)

1 Preheat oven to 375°. Lightly coat 15 × 10-inch jelly-roll pan with nonstick cooking spray.

2 Stand apples upright and carefully core each apple from top to within ½ inch of bottom. Cut ¼-inch-thin slice from top. Fill cavities with mixed dried fruit and dot with butter. Place 1 tablespoon apricot jam on top of each.

3 Place phyllo on clean, dry surface. Cover lightly with waxed paper and then with a slightly dampened towel, to prevent drying out.

4 Place sheet of waxed paper on work surface, and lift 1 sheet of phyllo onto waxed paper. Lightly coat with nonstick cooking spray. Place another sheet on top and again lightly coat. Stand 1 apple in center of phyllo. Lifting both sheets, bring one corner up and over top of apple and down other side. Repeat with other 3 corners so apple is completely covered, pressing phyllo against apple smoothly and securely. Place phyllo-covered apple in prepared pan and lightly coat with cooking spray. Repeat with remaining phyllo, more nonstick cooking spray, and apples.

5 Bake in 375° oven until phyllo is golden brown and apples are tender when pierced with a wooden pick, 30 to 35 minutes. Transfer pan to wire rack to cool, 10 to 15 minutes. Using spatula, transfer apples to dessert plates and halve each apple lengthwise using serrated knife. Serve warm, cut sides up, and pour any juices remaining in pan over apples. Dollop with reduced-fat sour cream and sprinkle with cinnamon, if you'd like.

NUTRIENT VALUE PER SERVING OF MY BAKED APPLE

331 calories, 4 g protein, 5 g fat (13% fat; 2 g saturated fat), 72 g carbohydrate, 191 mg sodium, 5 mg cholesterol

THE CLASSIC BAKED APPLE IN PUFF PASTRY

604 calories (almost twice as many calories), 27 g fat (4½ times the fat)

a is for . . .

There are three kinds of apples:
eating, baking, and all-purpose.
Most are available year-round
but are really at their best in
late summer and fall. To keep
apples crisp, store them in the
refrigerator or a cool dark place.
The best of the all-purpose are:
GRANNY SMITH (crisp, tart,
and green); **McINTOSH** (tart,
red to green); and **GOLDEN
DELICIOUS** (sweet and yellow).

Pineapple Dream Boat

MAKES 6 SERVINGS
(EACH REGULAR-SIZE PINEAPPLE HALF IS 3 SERVINGS)

PREP: 25 MINUTES, PLUS FREEZING AND CHILLING

COOK: 30 MINUTES

Move over, Carmen Miranda! This is not a hat. It's not a soufflé. And it's certainly no fool, because there's not a drop of heavy cream anywhere. This boat is piled high with just the most dreamy, fluffy mixture of fresh pineapple puree and beaten egg whites (see Powdered Egg Whites Are Not Just for the Army, opposite page). And depending on how cool you want to be, you can serve this very cold or frozen. As a special gift for your guests, use miniature pineapples for this recipe. You'll need 3 of them, and figure half a pineapple per serving.

1 ripe, golden sweet pineapple with crown (about
   3 pounds)
½ cup superfine sugar
¼ cup golden or light rum
2 teaspoons fresh lime juice
½ teaspoon coconut flavoring or extract
2 tablespoons powdered egg whites
6 tablespoons warm water
⅛ teaspoon cream of tartar

1 Halve pineapple lengthwise through crown. Using paring knife, cut out and discard core running down center of each pineapple half. Cut out pineapple from shell halves in large chunks and reserve (use a grapefruit knife, if you have one, since it cuts out the fruit more easily). With spoon, scrape out fruit and excess juice from bottoms of shells into 1-quart glass measure, leaving ¼-inch-thick pineapple boats, which will become serving containers. Blot boats with paper towel and place in freezer until frozen solid.

2 Cut large chunks of pineapple into ¼-inch pieces. Add to scraped pineapple pulp and juice in glass measure (you should have about 3 cups). In medium saucepan, combine pineapple mixture with ¼ cup sugar and the rum. Bring to a boil over high heat, stirring. Reduce heat to medium and boil mixture until liquid cooks off and pineapple pieces are glazed-looking, about 30 minutes, stirring occasionally. Transfer to small metal bowl. Stir in lime juice and coconut flavoring. Refrigerate mixture until very cold, about 2 hours.

3 In medium bowl, whisk together powdered egg whites and 6 tablespoons warm water until egg whites are completely dissolved, about 2 minutes. Add cream of tartar. With electric mixer on medium-high speed, beat until soft peaks form. Increase

mixer speed to high and beat in remaining ¼ cup sugar, 1 tablespoon at a time, until stiff and glossy peaks form.

4 Fold egg white mixture into chilled pineapple mixture. Spoon into frozen pineapple shells and serve immediately. If serving frozen, place filled pineapple shells in freezer for several hours or overnight until mixture is semi-hard (mixture will not freeze rock hard). Present in pineapple boats and spoon into dessert bowls.

NUTRIENT VALUE PER SERVING OF
MY DREAM BOAT

161 calories, 2 g protein, 1 g fat (6% fat; 0 g saturated fat),
31 g carbohydrate, 27 mg sodium, 0 mg cholesterol

FOR A DREAM BOAT WITH HEAVY CREAM
274 calories (almost twice the calories),
22 g fat (22 times the fat)

NOT A TIPSY BOAT

At first glance, it may look like there's a lot of alcohol in this recipe. You know I do not drink—I'm all natural. But don't worry about the alcohol—the cooking heat evaporates all the alcohol, leaving behind just a delicious, tropical flavor.

powdered egg whites are not just for the army

Now don't get scared, but the U.S. Department of Agriculture and other organizations recommend that you not use uncooked eggs in anything, and that includes uncooked meringues made from egg whites. So, there go the egg whites. Send them to me—I use them on my face! My trick for this meringue filling is powdered egg whites, easily found in the baking aisle of your supermarket.

I sometimes think I'd like to know
Just when I'm going to die,
So I could eat such favorite foods
As Peanut Butter Pie.

Catering my final meal,
I'd set with detailed care
A groaning endless table
That would be a grand affair.

When I hand in my knife and fork
the very final time,
I want to know I've had it all,
From simple to sublime.

So here it is, my favorite list,
And just before I go
I'll savor every special dish
All laid out in a row.

But just in case I stay a while,
The final feast delayed,
I'll taste small portions now and then,
All other action stayed.

I'll summon all my discipline
'Cause even through my sighs,
I know I'm not prepared to wear
These dishes on my thighs.

You Can't Take It With You

Peanut Butter Meringue Pie

MAKES 10 SERVINGS

PREP: 30 MINUTES, PLUS CHILLING

COOK: 7 MINUTES

BAKE: CRUST AT 425° FOR 10 TO 12
MINUTES; PIE AT 325° FOR ABOUT
5 MINUTES

Have you done this? You open your cupboard. You take out a jar of peanut butter. You unscrew the top. You take your index finger, dip it in the jar, scoop out a huge wad of peanut butter, and then walk around the house eating it. If preferred, this can also be done with a spoon. This is peanut butter at its most primitive. Well, buckle in. With this recipe, I take peanut butter to a place were no jar has ever been before—a meringue pie!

CRUST

1½ cups all-purpose flour

¼ teaspoon salt

½ cup solid vegetable shortening, chilled (or, ¼ cup
   unsalted butter + ¼ cup solid vegetable shortening)

3 to 4 tablespoons cold water

FILLING

¾ cup confectioners' sugar

½ cup peanut butter, smooth or crunchy

2 cups milk

½ cup granulated sugar

¼ cup cornstarch

¼ teaspoon salt

3 large egg yolks

2 tablespoons unsalted butter, at room temperature

½ teaspoon pure vanilla extract

MERINGUE

3 large egg whites, at room temperature

3 tablespoons granulated sugar

1. Preheat oven to 425°.

2. *Make crust:* In medium bowl, stir together flour and salt. With pastry blender, 2 knives held like scissors, or your fingertips, cut in shortening until mixture resembles coarse meal. Gradually sprinkle in 3 to 4 tablespoons cold water, tossing with fork, until dough comes together. Shape into disk. On lightly floured waxed paper, roll out dough to 11-inch circle. Invert waxed paper with dough into 9-inch pie dish. Remove waxed paper. Fit dough into dish. Crimp edges.

3. Bake crust in 425° oven until lightly golden, 10 to 12 minutes. Transfer to wire rack to cool slightly.

4. *Meanwhile, make filling:* In medium bowl, with pastry blender or 2 knives held like scissors, cut confectioners' sugar into peanut butter until mixture resembles coarse meal. Sprinkle half of mixture over bottom of slightly cooled pie crust and reserve remainder.

5. In medium saucepan, heat milk over medium heat until bubbles appear around edges. Remove from heat.

6. In medium bowl, stir together granulated sugar, cornstarch, and salt. Gradually stir in hot milk.

7. In medium, heatproof bowl, with electric mixer on medium speed, beat egg yolks until pale yellow. Gradually stir in hot milk mixture. Place bowl over

simmering water in saucepan, without bottom of bowl touching water. Cook, stirring constantly, until thickened, about 7 minutes. Remove from heat. Stir in butter and vanilla. Pour filling into pie crust. Cool to room temperature. Press plastic wrap directly on surface of filling. Refrigerate until thoroughly chilled and firm, 1 to 2 hours.

8 *Just before serving, make meringue:* Preheat oven to 325°. In large bowl, with electric mixer on medium speed, beat egg whites until foamy. Gradually beat in sugar, 1 tablespoon at a time, until stiff and glossy

peaks form. Spread meringue over top of chilled pie filling, making sure meringue touches crust all around edges, sealing completely. Sprinkle top with reserved peanut butter mixture.

9 Bake in 325° oven until meringue is lightly golden, about 5 minutes. Transfer to wire rack to cool. Cut and serve.

NUTRIENT VALUE PER SERVING

402 calories, 9 g protein, 22 g fat (49% fat; 7 g saturated fat), 44 g carbohydrate, 212 mg sodium, 77 mg cholesterol

Crème de la Crème Brûlée

MAKES 6 INDIVIDUAL CUSTARDS

PREP: 20 MINUTES, PLUS STANDING
AND CHILLING

BAKE: AT 325° FOR 45 TO 50 MINUTES

BROIL: 1 MINUTE PER CUSTARD

I made my first trip to Paris when I was an art student in Florence. As soon as I had checked into my *pension*, I headed for the nearest brasserie, leaving a trail of pastry crumbs just to make sure I could find my way back. The restaurant was huge, and packed with people. A waiter in a black tie and white apron ran past carrying an enormous tray—but not before I got a look. The tray was stacked with these little soufflé cups. They were individual custards topped with a glistening gold crust that looked like ice. I was shown to a corner booth. "Garçon, bring me one of those custards. Well, maybe two." It was a *crème brûlée* [krehm broo-LAY]. In French it means "burnt cream," but it's not really burnt. The topping is brown sugar, which has been caramelized under a salamander—a fancy name for a broiler. You know the French. When I left, you couldn't see the top of my table—it was covered with empty soufflé cups. *Tip:* When you make *my* recipe, invite five friends over—no one should eat more than one of these.

2 cups heavy cream

½ cup milk

1½ teaspoons pure vanilla extract

5 large egg yolks

½ cup granulated sugar

Pinch salt

Boiling water

5 tablespoons superfine sugar

1. In small saucepan, stir together cream and milk. Heat just to simmering. Stir in vanilla. Remove from heat. Cover and let stand for 20 minutes.

2. Preheat oven to 325°. Place six 4-ounce ramekins or custard cups in 13 × 9 × 2-inch baking pan.

3. In small bowl, whisk together egg yolks, granulated sugar, and salt. Gently stir into cream mixture. Strain through fine-mesh sieve into a 4-cup glass measure. Pour into ramekins, dividing equally. Place baking pan on oven rack. Add enough boiling water to pan to come halfway up sides of ramekins.

4. Bake in 325° oven until custards are set around edge, and knife inserted near edge comes out clean but centers are still jiggly, 45 to 50 minutes. Remove ramekins from water to wire rack to cool. Cover with plastic wrap and refrigerate until thoroughly chilled.

5. Preheat broiler. With paper towels, blot top of each custard dry. Sprinkle 2½ teaspoons superfine sugar over custard in each ramekin to evenly cover top. Place 2 or 3 ramekins on small baking sheet.

6. Broil 4 inches from heat, rotating baking sheet often, until sugar is caramelized, about 1 minute. Remove, and repeat with remaining sugar and custards. Let stand until sugar hardens. Serve warm or chilled. (Can be refrigerated for up to 1 hour after caramelizing.)

NUTRIENT VALUE PER MY INDIVIDUAL CUSTARD

440 calories, 5 g protein, 34 g fat (69% fat; 20 g saturated fat), 30 g carbohydrate, 90 mg sodium, 289 mg cholesterol

Pecan Pralines

MAKES ABOUT 30 PRALINES

PREP: 45 MINUTES

COOK: ABOUT 20 MINUTES

When I was ten, I used to work for Leah's, the praline shop in the French Quarter in New Orleans—it's still there. As people lined up outside the shop, I walked by with a tray of broken pralines, offering them samples as a tease. The whole scene could have been a Charles Dickens movie. In fact, there was a photo of me doing this, which appeared in *National Geographic*. Even at an early age, my face was in magazines! The pralines I've created here are the old-fashioned honey-brown Creole-style kind.

1 cup granulated sugar

1 cup packed light-brown sugar

1 cup light cream

2 tablespoons corn syrup

½ teaspoon baking soda

1 tablespoon butter

2 cups pecan halves, toasted

1 Line 2 baking sheets with parchment paper. In heavy 3-quart saucepan, combine both sugars, cream, corn syrup, and baking soda, until blended. Bring to boil over medium-low heat, stirring with wooden spoon to prevent scorching. Cook until mixture reaches soft-ball stage (240° on candy or deep-fat frying thermometer).

2 Remove from heat. Stir in butter and then pecans. Beat with wooden spoon until mixture thickens slightly (temperature should be about 210° to 220°).

Drop onto prepared baking sheets by tablespoonfuls to form 2½-inch-diameter pralines. (This is the tricky part, deciding when they can be dropped. If you wait too long, they will not flatten out and will start to crystallize. You may want to do a few test candies. You can rewarm the mixture if it hasn't cooled too much; place over low heat and stir as little as possible.) Let candies harden, and store between sheets of waxed paper in airtight container.

NUTRIENT VALUE PER MY PRALINE

123 calories, 1 g protein, 8 g fat (54% fat; 2 g saturated fat), 14 g carbohydrate, 27 mg sodium, 10 mg cholesterol

CHECK THE WEATHER

As with most candies, you want to make sure the weather is going to be dry and cool when you make these—or so the experts say. Otherwise, they may never harden. But you know, there are not many places more humid than New Orleans, and there they always seem to be perfect.

pecans tip the scale

You may have noticed that I don't use pecans anywhere in this book, except in this chapter. Why do you think that is? You guessed it. They have a higher fat content than any other nut—more than 70 percent! That's why you should keep them refrigerated—to avoid rancidity. By the way, in case you were wondering about the pecan's pedigree, it's a native American and a member of the hickory family.

Tiramisù

MAKES 10 SERVINGS

PREP: 20 MINUTES, PLUS CHILLING

At first I thought this was an Italian race car. "Oh, look! There goes a Lamborghini! And right behind it there's a Tiramisù! What a pretty blue color." I was so embarrassed when I found out it was an Italian dessert. It's luscious layers of whipped cream mixed with buttery mascarpone cheese, and ladyfingers flavored with coffee. So, when you're ready to toast dessert, raise your forks and repeat after me, in an Italian accent, "Here's to tiramisù, and to you, and to you, and to you!"

8 ounces mascarpone cheese
⅓ cup granulated sugar
3 tablespoons coffee liqueur
1 teaspoon pure vanilla extract
1½ cups heavy cream
24 ladyfingers (7-ounce package)
1 cup strong brewed coffee
3 ounces semisweet chocolate, grated (about 1 cup)
1 tablespoon confectioners' sugar

1 In large bowl, with electric mixer on medium-low speed, beat together mascarpone cheese and granulated sugar. Beat in coffee liqueur and vanilla.

2 In medium bowl, with electric mixer on medium speed, beat cream until stiff peaks form. Fold whipped cream into mascarpone mixture.

3 In glass baking dish just large enough to hold half the ladyfingers in one layer, about 11 × 7 inches, arrange half the ladyfingers over bottom. Sprinkle them with half the coffee. Spoon half the mascarpone mixture over ladyfingers. Sprinkle with half the grated chocolate. Arrange remaining ladyfingers over mascarpone layer. Sprinkle with remaining coffee. Spoon remaining mascarpone mixture on top. Sprinkle with remaining grated chocolate.

4 Cover and refrigerate at least 4 hours, preferably overnight.

5 Sprinkle with confectioners' sugar before serving.

NUTRIENT VALUE PER SERVING
384 calories, 5 g protein, 28 g fat (64% fat; 10 g saturated fat), 28 g carbohydrate, 56 mg sodium, 150 mg cholesterol

TIRAMISÙ MEANS WHAT?

The word *tiramisù*, in Italian, means "carry me up" or "pick me up." This dessert is so ethereal, it really is like riding a cloud up to heaven. By the way, it's pronounced tir-rah-me-SOO.

mascarpone

No, it's not a new dance. Mascarpone (mas-cahr-POHN-ay) is a rich Italian cheese made from cow's milk, with the texture of a very thick heavy cream. It's a delicious dessert on its own, topped with a little fresh fruit. But remember what chapter you're in!

ladyfingers

Ladyfingers look like you know what . . . that's how they get their name. They come soft and spongy, or hard and crisp. Take your pick. Once they soak up the coffee and the mascarpone, they get deliciously mushy anyway.

Cashews Galore Fudge Bars

MAKES 36 BARS

PREP: 20 MINUTES, PLUS CHILLING

BAKE: CASHEWS AT 350° FOR 8 MINUTES

At parties, we've all stood by the dish of mixed cocktail nuts and, when no one was looking, quickly picked out the cashews. Or, there's the other trick. When the coast is clear, we take the can of cocktail nuts, spread the nuts out on the kitchen counter, pick out all the cashews, and then return the rest of the nuts to the can. So, to honor all cashew-pickers everywhere, I've created the ultimate fudge. And guess what? It's loaded with cashews.

Nonstick vegetable-oil cooking spray

1 ⅓ cups cashews, very coarsely chopped

1 can (14 ounces) sweetened condensed milk

2 cups coarsely chopped semisweet chocolate

2 ounces unsweetened chocolate, chopped

1 teaspoon pure vanilla extract

1. Preheat oven to 350°. Line 8 × 8 × 2-inch square baking pan with aluminum foil. Lightly coat with nonstick cooking spray. Spread cashews on baking sheet.

2. Bake cashews in 350° oven, stirring occasionally, until fragrant, about 8 minutes.

3. In medium, heavy saucepan, bring condensed milk to simmering over low heat, stirring constantly. Remove from heat. Add both chocolates, cover, and let stand 5 minutes. Stir until smooth. Stir in 1 cup cashews and the vanilla. Scrape into prepared baking pan, spreading in an even layer. Sprinkle on remaining ⅓ cup cashews, pressing lightly into fudge to adhere.

4. Cover and refrigerate until firm, at least 2 hours. Cut into 36 squares. Store in airtight container, refrigerated. Serve at room temperature.

NUTRIENT VALUE PER MY FUDGE BAR

117 calories, 2 g protein, 7 g fat (49 % fat; 3 g saturated fat), 14 g carbohydrate, 45 mg sodium, 4 mg cholesterol

where does the cashew come from?

No, not a blue can. Ready for this? It comes from the cashew apple tree. Mother Nature is so funny. The nut, which grows from the bottom of the pear-shaped apple, has a shell that is very thick—"If I had a hammer, I'd hammer . . ."—and very poisonous. Who would have guessed that something so delicious . . . ? But once the nut is taken out of its shell, it's okay. It's a happy nut, shaped like a smile. Its buttery flavor is perfect for my fudge. And I'm not going to tell you that it's one of the fattiest nuts at 48 percent fat. But please, cut the fudge into small pieces.

 Celebration Cake

MAKES 24 SERVINGS

Any time there's a celebration, you always ask people what kind of cake they want. Here I present to you the universal celebration cake, for when you care to serve the very best. It rises to any occasion: a birthday, anniversary, Chinese New Year, buying a new refrigerator, whatever. I've kept mine basic white, just like a wedding dress. To me, that's very elegant. But if you want stripes, colors, jellybeans, or plastic animals, that's okay. So go have a party! One word of warning—don't leave bowls of the frosting sitting out, or you'll be serving a plain cake!

Unsalted butter, for greasing pans
Cake flour, for dusting pans

CAKES

8 ounces blanched slivered almonds (1¾ cups)
2 cups + 2 tablespoons cake flour
1 tablespoon + ½ teaspoon baking powder
10 tablespoons (1¼ sticks) unsalted butter, at room temperature
2 cups granulated sugar
5 large eggs, separated
1 tablespoon pure vanilla extract
¼ teaspoon almond extract
¾ cup + 1 tablespoon milk
¼ teaspoon cream of tartar

1 recipe White Chocolate Frosting (page 187), chilled
1 pint fresh raspberries

1 Make cakes: Preheat oven to 350°. Grease 7 × 2-inch round layer-cake pan, and 9 × 9 × 2-inch square cake pan. Dust pans with flour, tapping out excess. Spread almonds on baking sheet.

2 Bake almonds in 350° oven, stirring frequently, until golden and fragrant, 8 to 10 minutes. Let cool. In a food processor, grind nuts with on/off pulses until very fine. Be careful not to overprocess, or you'll have a nut paste.

3 In medium bowl, stir together flour, baking powder, and ground almonds.

4 In large bowl, with electric mixer on medium speed, beat butter until smooth. Beat in sugar until light and fluffy. Add egg yolks, one at a time, beating well after each addition. Add vanilla and almond extracts and beat until blended.

5 Reduce mixer speed to low. Alternately beat flour mixture and milk into butter mixture in three additions, beginning and ending with flour mixture, beating well after each addition.

6 In clean medium bowl, with clean beaters, beat egg whites with cream of tartar on medium-low until soft peaks form. Fold one-third of whites into batter. Gently fold in remaining whites, being careful not to overmix batter. Pour batter into prepared pans.

continued

7 Bake in 350° oven until a wooden pick inserted in centers comes out clean, 35 to 45 minutes. Cool cakes in pans on wire racks for 10 minutes. Invert cakes onto wire racks. Remove pans. Let cool completely.

8 *To assemble:* Have well-chilled White Chocolate Frosting ready and waiting in the refrigerator. Place cooled cake layers on clean work surface. With long serrated knife, cut each cake in half horizontally. Place bottom half of square cake, cut side up, on platter or foil-covered piece of heavy cardboard. Spread top evenly with ½ cup tinted frosting. Arrange half the raspberries over top. Spread with another ½ cup tinted frosting. Gently place top half of square cake, cut side down, on top. With metal spatula, spread any oozing frosting evenly against sides of cake. Spread ⅓ cup tinted frosting over rounded surface of one half of round cake. Place, frosted side down, in center of square cake. Spread top with ⅓ cup tinted frosting. Place remaining raspberries over top. Spread with remaining tinted frosting. Cover with top half of round cake, cut side down. Spread any oozing frosting evenly against side of cake.

9 Using small metal spatula, spread untinted frosting over entire cake (both tiers) in thin layer. Then frost entire cake with thicker layer. Decorate as pictured or as desired, using a pastry bag fitted with different tips. Refrigerate until serving time. Let come to room temperature to serve.

NUTRIENT VALUE PER SERVING

503 calories, 7 g protein, 36 g fat (63% fat; 19 g saturated fat), 41 g carbohydrate, 110 mg sodium, 130 mg cholesterol

the three faces of almonds

You can buy almonds whole, sliced, or slivered. Whole are good for garnishing and grinding. Both sliced and slivered are excellent "as is" in baking. The nuts come either in their skins, which makes them slightly bitter-tasting, or naked (a.k.a. blanched), without the skin and sweeter-tasting. Two other wonderful qualitites you should know about: Almonds are high in vitamin E and are on the low end of the fat-scale for nuts.

White Chocolate Frosting

PREP: 30 MINUTES, PLUS CHILLING

I make the frosting in two batches so I don't have to use a huge bowl. Plus this way, the smaller amounts are easier to work with and they chill faster.

2½ cups + 2½ cups heavy cream
  8 ounces + another 8 ounces good-quality
    white chocolate, chopped
  Red food coloring

1 In medium saucepan, heat ½ cup heavy cream (from first 2½ cup batch) to boiling over medium heat. Remove from heat. Add 8 ounces chopped white chocolate and whisk until melted and thoroughly blended. Pour into large bowl, and place in refrigerator until thoroughly chilled, but not hardened, about 1 to 2 hours. Also chill beaters and 2 cups heavy cream in refrigerator. Clean and dry saucepan. Repeat with remaining cream and chocolate, combining ½ cup cream and 8 ounces chocolate and chilling remaining 2 cups cream. Keep batches separate.

2 Working with the two batches, add 2 cups chilled cream to *each* batch of chilled chocolate mixture. With electric mixer on medium-high speed with chilled beaters, beat each mixture until soft peaks form. Frosting should look like whipped cream. Do not overbeat.

3 Remove 2 cups frosting to clean bowl. Tint pink with few drops red food coloring. Refrigerate frostings to chill and thicken.

NUTRIENT VALUE PER SERVING
272 calories, 2 g protein, 24 g fat (78% fat; 15 g saturated fat), 13 g carbohydrate, 35 mg sodium, 72 mg cholesterol

Index

fondue, 154
  fondue with fruit, dippity-
    doo-da, 154–55
fortune cookies (seek your
  fortune, cookie), 50–51
frostings:
  cream cheese, 71
  molasses, 67
  rainbow, 83
  vanilla, 84
  white, 88–89
  white chocolate, 187
frozen desserts, 114–28
  casa blanca cake, 124–25
  ice, very nice, 118
  melon trio, the 116–17
  meringue "ice cream"
    sandwiches, 126–27
  pink-and-white velvet
    semifreddo, 122–23
  pink ice granita, 120–21
  pink-tie-only frozen soufflé,
    128–29
  sherbet, 117
  sorbet, 117
  sundae, five-minute, 119
fruit:
  complex carbohydrates in, 12
  dried, 21
  see also specific fruits
fruit desserts, 148–71
  apple-cranberry crumble,
    152–53
  baked apple, uptown, 168–69
  cherry-pear cobblers,
    Martha's, 158–59
  cobbler, cozy, 150–51
  crepes à la Barbra, 160–61
  cutting up with Mother
    Nature, 166–67
  fondue with fruit, dippity-
    doo-da, 154–55
  hey, sucker!, 162–63
  peaches, Georgia baked
    stuffed, 156–57
  pineapple dream boat,
    170–71
  tartlets, my little, 94–95
  waffles with blackberry-
    nectarine sauce, World's
    Fair, 164–65
fudge bars, cashews galore,
  182–83

G

gems, walnut–sour cream,
  66–67
Georgia baked stuffed peaches,
  156–57
ginger-almond biscotti,
  30–31
gingersnap cookies:
  in Georgia baked stuffed
    peaches, 156–57
glazes:
  chocolate, 96–97, 139–40
  orange, 63
  tangerine or orange, 76
  two-tone, 87
graham cracker(s):
  in pie crust, 93, 99
  in some more s'mores,
    48–49
granita(s), 120
  grapefruit (pink ice granita),
    120–21
  melon (the melon trio),
    116–17
  pink ice granita, 120–21
grapefruit:
  in pink ice granita, 120–21
grapenuts cereal:
  in have you Athena baklava?,
    68–69
grapes:
  in cutting up with Mother
    Nature, 166–67

H

have you Athena baklava?,
  68–69
hazelnut(s), 19
  chocolate-hazelnut biscotti,
    28–29
  in "I do, I do" wedding
    cookies, 52–53
hearts:
  chocolate, 93
  watermelon, 167
heavy cream, 13
hey, sucker!, 162–63
honey, 12, 14, 15
  in very nice ice, 118
honeydew:
  in cutting up with Mother
    Nature, 166–67
  in the melon trio, 116–17

I

ice(s):
  berry (very nice ice), 118
  grapefruit (pink ice granita),
    120–21
  melon (the melon trio),
    116–17
icing:
  orange, 80
  see also frostings
"I do, I do" wedding cookies,
  52–53
igloo cake (casa blanca cake),
  124–25
"I'm late, I'm late" carrot cake,
  70–71
ingredients, 14–21
  butter, 13, 14, 17, 33, 53, 60
  buttermilk, 13, 15, 84, 87,
    110
  chocolate, 13, 20, 92
  cocoa powder, 20, 84, 92
  cream cheese, 39
  dairy products, 15–16
  dried fruit, 21
  eggs, 14, 18–19, 84, 87, 171
  flour, 20, 95
  lemon juice, 99, 103
  natural fat substitutes, 18
  nondairy whipped topping,
    17
  nuts, 19, 31, 52, 69, 79, 178,
    182, 186
  oils, 17–18, 51, 60
  phyllo, 21
  solid spreads, 17
  sweeteners, 14–15
  yogurt, 16, 60
I-thought-it-was-a-hot-dog
  cannoli cookie, 38–39
it's a fine-lime pound cake,
  60–61

J

Josephine's napoleon, 146–47

K

keep on truckin' brownies,
  36–37
kisses, sealed with a kiss, 34–35
  cocoa, 35
  mint, 35
  orange, 35
  strawberry, 35
  vanilla-almond, 34–35
kiwifruit:
  in mama mia! a brownie
    pizza!, 40–41
  in the royal trifle, 142–44
  sauce (for rice pudding), 132

L

ladyfingers, 181
  in tiramisù, 180–81
layer cake, easy-iced chocolate,
  80–81
leaves, chocolate, 93
lemon:
  lemon bars, diamond, 26–27
  lemon lollipops (hey, sucker!),
    162
  lemon merenga pie, 98–99
  in Madeleine's cake-cookies,
    32–33
lime:
  fine-lime pound cake, it's a,
    60–61
  lime bars, 27
Linzer sandwich cookies (to
    Linzer, with love), 42–43
little crown cakes, 86–87
  chocolate, 87
littlest angel cakes, the,
    88–89
lollipops (hey, sucker!), 162–63
  blue mint, 162
  cherry, 162
  coconut, 162
  lemon, 162
  orange, 163
  strawberry, 162
lost-in-Boston cream pie, 96–97
low-fat and low-calorie, 11

M

macadamia nuts, 19
Madeleine's cake-cookies,
  32–33
mama mia! a brownie pizza!,
  40–41
maple syrup, 14
  in Cinderella pumpkin pie,
    94–95
marshmallow(s), 37, 135
  in keep on truckin' brownies,
    36–37